ANIMAL
SPIRIT GUIDES

ANIMAL
SPIRIT GUIDES

Discover your power animal
and the shamanic path

CHRIS LÜTTICHAU

CICO BOOKS

LONDON NEW YORK

Power coming
is a feeling
of sleep ending
and being beginning.

The Dream Spirits

Published in 2009 by CICO Books
An imprint of Ryland Peters & Small
20–21 Jockey's Fields   519 Broadway, 5th Floor
London WC1R 4BW   New York, NY 10012
www.cicobooks.com

10 9 8 7 6 5 4 3 2 1

Text © Chris Lüttichau 2009
Design and illustrations © CICO Books 2009

A CIP catalog record for this book is available from the Library of Congress
and the British Library.

ISBN 978 1 906525 54 5

Design: Roger Hammond, bluegumdesigners.com
Illustration and cover illustration: Melissa Launay

Printed in China

CONTENTS

BEGINNING YOUR JOURNEY

THE PURPOSE OF the teachings in this book is for you to discover whether they feel true for you. Find out if they awaken a remembrance within yourself and your body of an ancient instinctual bond between you, nature, and animals.

Teachings that were passed on to me stressed one crucial principle: never give away your self-respect and self-authority, whether to a book, a teacher, a partner, a religion, a church, a job, or anything else. No one can tell you what to think or what to do—a principle that applies to this book. What I write about animals and their medicine is simply based on what my teachers have shown me, on my own observations, my dreams and personal insights. I don't claim this to be the ultimate truth. Animals and animal spirits should not be defined in ways that limit and restrict. No one can tell you how things are, as this is between you and the highest power. This knowledge is the first step in understanding animal medicines.

One aspect of working spiritually is that you are investing in yourself, and consequently you can expect a yield of some kind. This book contains a series of methods and exercises in how to work with animal spirits. If you choose to use these methods sincerely, you invest in yourself and in your future. It is my experience that these practices improve your life, not just in the context of a current situation and short-term goals, but also in the long term. In the words of one of my teachers: "Animal spirits can help us become better human beings."

✦ Unique Lessons ✦

The title of this book refers to the medicine, or power, that is unique to each species of animal. When observing animals carefully, we find that each species has a gift that differentiates it from others. If you want to discover the medicine of a particular animal, study that animal and look for what is distinctive about it. There is always at least one quality or behavioral trait that is unique to each species. For the deer it is a particular combination of magic, gentleness, and alertness. For the hummingbird, it is joy, beauty, and responsibility. Once we can begin to realize that each animal brings a lesson, and we are willing to learn from animals, an astonishing school of wisdom opens up to us. In the days when there were no universities or books, when culture was passed down through generations orally, native people learned from nature, which was their source of knowledge. Everything they needed to know could be learned from trees, plants, animals, rivers, the seasons, the Sun, Moon, and stars.

There is almost no limit to what we, too, can learn in the same way. Water, for example, teaches us about our emotions. It can be clear, calm, and life-giving, but at other times the winds of change can create turbulence—waves hit the shore, and every now and then a storm builds, resulting in destruction and even death. Our emotions are similar: sometimes they nurture us, letting us experience joy and love, now and then we can feel sad and angry, and at times jealousy or rage may take over and destroy relationships.

✦ The Magical Mirror ✦

Life is a mirror, and everything around us is here to teach us, if we are willing to look into it. I learned early on my path to recognize that the whole of life is a field of learning, where we discover what we need to know about ourselves and what it is like to be human, existing in the physical dimension. Looking into the Magical Mirror of life, we can see the truth and all the wisdom of the universe. Reality has many different layers, and things are not necessarily what they appear to be. What meets the eye is just the surface of what is, and our journey as human beings involves an eventual unveiling of the teachings that are hidden all around us.

✦ The Mind and the Heart ✦

Illusions are the nature of the world, and the mind tends to accept things for what they seem to be on the surface. The rational mind is a brilliant resource that is part of our medicine as human beings, but it is just one of our powers. We need to guard against it taking sole charge as it is predisposed to create a maze of random thoughts in which we are easily lost. To see through illusions we must access other faculties, because the mind always seeks to categorize, to name, and to decide that its knowledge is definitive. In this, the mind can be deceptive. It is the heart that helps us to look into the Magical Mirror and to understand its teachings. The mind speculates; the heart knows.

In the center of every human being is the heart—the seat of our Sacred Self. This is where we ultimately go to find answers and to make choices in our lives. Your Sacred Self is your ultimate authority. It is the eternal part, a divine spark, within every one of us. This place needs always to be respected and remembered. If we give away our power to others we do not honor who we truly are or follow our own path. We are all born to learn and to make our own choices as we walk the path of life. To be real, choices need to come from free will. It is essential that we honor our free will if we want to be true to ourselves.

Choice is one of the medicines of the human being. Animals also

have choice, but not to the extent that we do. Most animals mate only at certain times during the year, they usually respond to danger with either fight or flight, they live in specific habitats, and eat a certain variety of food. Our multitude of choices sets us apart, but is accompanied by responsibility. Each choice we make has a consequence for which we are responsible.

Every one of us can make the choice to walk a path of self-respect and self-authority. This is our right as human beings. We do not need to be born into a certain tribe or belong to a particular culture—in our souls we are all native people, native to the land and to the Earth. We are spirits born into substance to learn and grow; we all emerge from the same source and ultimately return there. Separation is an illusion, but it is a persistent and convincing one that feeds directly into the nature of the mind and how it interprets reality. This is one of the reasons why animal spirits have so much to offer us and teach us. They are not caught in the illusions of the mind, and they do not have big egos. They perceive from a deep inner place of knowing, from the center of who they are—from the heart. They can show us how to find that place within ourselves. When we arrive there, we become genuine.

To become a genuine human is a high art. It requires dedication to find the way back to your center. Forgetfulness of who we really are leads us away from our center, and into the maze of the mind. Forgetfulness is part of the challenge of the human condition, and it takes hold during childhood. We need a remedy so, like a big cat, we may begin to hunt ourselves and find the trail back to our remembrance and our power. My teachers gave me the tools to do this. They had been given these tools by their teachers in a long lineage of those who pass on oral wisdom. In this book, you too will find the tools for your journey.

As we walk this path, we must stop and listen to the hushed voices behind us—the voices of our ancestors, the keepers of these teachings. They speak softly and their voices can be easily drowned by the noise of our own thoughts. Take the time to be in quietness, listening to the ancient voices carried in the wind.

My Personal Journey

I studied for more than 20 years, mainly in North America, to learn the ways of animal medicine and other related teachings, mostly from native teachers who were willing to share what they knew. They told me to study nature and learn directly from animals, trees, mountains, lakes, and rivers. I welcomed these instructions, because they resonated with me. I have had an enthusiasm for meeting wild animals and learning about them since I was a child. Each time I saw an animal I had not seen before, it was an adventure and a gift. My first meetings with different animals, including a coyote, bear, rattlesnake, pine marten, bald eagle, and hummingbird, to mention a few, are still clearly imprinted in my mind. This is not just due to the beauty and harmony of such animals, but because of the mysterious power they express. They know things we humans do not. They all continue to teach me, making my life rich and exciting.

Since then I have also learned from a European teacher who showed me that the more esoteric aspects of the teachings on animal medicine, which I thought had been lost or hidden away by those who had decided to keep the teachings to themselves, are still accessible. She showed me the concealed path to uncovering them. This discovery filled me with joy because I realized that nothing is truly lost, and believing so is an illusion.

Now I invite you to join me on a journey of adventure into the realm of the animal spirits. I invite you to look into the Magical Mirror of Animal Medicine and let your heart be your guide.

→ PART ONE →

THE PATH

In the following chapters you will find an introduction to discovering your power animal as well as methods of working with one you may already have. Each of us can connect with animal spirit guides and find our power animal, which offers energy, or medicine (see the animal profiles in Chapter 4, page 58). Included are exercises on calling your animal into a dream, working with power objects to maintain contact with your animal, and embarking on drum journeys.

CHAPTER ONE

FINDING YOUR ANIMAL SPIRIT GUIDE

✦ The Power Animal ✦

In essence, an animal spirit guide, or power animal, is a guardian spirit. However, as well as being our protector, it has several other roles. As the name implies, a power animal helps us find our own inner strength, which comes from knowing who we are and being "centered." Linked to this is a sense of being connected to the rest of creation in a healthy, balanced way that enhances our own life and that of others. Not only do we then function well in the physical reality of our everyday lives, but we have a direct and strong connection to the spiritual world.

A power animal helps you to walk a strong path where you manifest your true self and are of good service to others during your life. This means following a path that allows you to continue to grow in understanding and expand your awareness of all that life is. You must trust yourself and your own power while maintaining humility, and be willing to own and transform the distorted sides of the self, such as self-importance, limiting fears, and negative projections. Connecting to your power animal also implies living in accordance with the natural laws under the guidance of the Creator, the Great Spirit, the Divine, or whatever term you prefer to describe the highest power. Living in this way is true power, and it has nothing to do with controlling others. The power animal is your protector, friend, and companion on this path.

The power animal as your mirror

As your spirit helper and guardian, your power animal exists outside yourself, but it can also be seen as a reflection of who you are. The way you walk and talk, your body language, habits, demeanor, and appearance are all like those of your power animal. It is therefore possible to learn to see someone's power animal just by looking at that person and noticing their behavior and appearance.

For example, someone with hawk as a power animal might have a certain detachment in the way they tend to view the world. Such a person might prefer to live on the upper floors of a building or sit in the upper rows of a theatre, for example; he or she may have a sharp eye for detail, and even possess a certain fierceness. The hawk will also be reflected in their face and in their general appearance. Likewise, people with bear as a power animal will have a similar walk and posture to a bear. This makes them appear strong and grounded. One of my teachers, a Native American, told me the reason why you have this likeness is that you have been your power animal in a past life. The union between humans and their power animals is reflected in many of the ancient mythologies, from Greek to Native American, where gods and goddesses appear in various animal forms: as a salmon, a swan, or a white buffalo.

The merging of humans and animals also reflects the fact that deep, spiritual work by humanity has always involved merging with animal spirits, for the simple fact that they have abilities we don't. On a basic level, for instance, their senses are in most cases superior to ours. Animals and humans are made of the same material, and union results in more than exists when the two are separate.

The nature of power animals

Power animals warn us of danger, protect us from it, and awaken sleeping powers within us. Our health improves when they are near, since they affect our immune system. When we have made a real connection with our power animals, we can begin to feel grounded and safe in our bodies, becoming more comfortable with the world around us. Power animals help us to find our confidence with people and guide us home to ourselves. Once they are with us, we are never alone.

In a sense the connection to a power animal is very similar to the phenomenon experienced by many people in love: an energetic link is established to the loved one so that, for example, you can feel when he or she is approaching.

It doesn't matter if the energy in this connection is physical or metaphysical, it can be understood as the same energy. This understanding resonates in the hearts and the minds of many people, and is supported by discoveries in quantum physics, with its concept of non-locality: the world is host to an invisible reality which allows non-mediated communication to happen faster than the speed of light, despite separation over great distances. An example of this could be extra-sensory perception, one of the traditional skills of the shaman. Some of the exercises described in this book are about training your ability to perceive in this way.

From a shaman's perspective, nothing really dies. When an animal's life ends, the spirit survives and leaves the physical body behind on earth, just like the spirit of a human being. Some of these spirits become power animals. According to the teachings I have received, humans are usually born again as humans, but not always. You can come back as a

raccoon, for example. From a spiritual perspective, animals are people just like you and I, only in animal guise. This is why native people refer to them as relatives, brothers, and sisters.

In our DNA we are very similar to animals. In mythology, where humans and animals speak the same language and sometimes form close bonds, our lives are intertwined. Human beings see and then rationalize what they see, but animals see and experience directly—their perception is not colored by a rational mind. Animals are clairvoyant on a different level than is manifest in some humans. The clairvoyance of animals works on a more instinctual level. They can't send an SMS, but they have empathy, they can grieve, and they are emotional like we are. They have a consciousness, and they have access to the divine. Power animals make wonderful allies as spirits.

In this book I distinguish between power animals and animal spirits in general. When using the term power animal I refer to your guardian spirit, the one who is also your mirror. Other animal spirits might well help you with different tasks, but your closest connection is with your power animal. This distinction is for the

Above and opposite: Animal spirit guides in general and our personal power animal can guide us forward on our path through life.

purpose of clarity, and is not necessarily how others would explain it.

Shamanism and spiritual reality

The teachings given here about power animals are closely linked to the shamanic tradition. Shamanism does not constitute a religion, but is a spiritual path without dogma, and it gives each human being the freedom to explore reality with an open mind and heart and to find her or his own truths.

Shamanism is about perceiving and knowing reality with as much clarity as possible. By reality, I mean the physical world as well as the realm of spirit. The ancient peoples of separate continents would not have had frequent contact with one another, and yet shamans all round the world have perceived existence in very much the same way. In their concepts of power animals and spirit guides, all shamans use psychic abilities to perceive spiritual realms as accurately as they can. Through the centuries, shamans have observed a reality in which all that exists is animated. This means that everything has consciousness and a soul, and is therefore alive even though, as with a stone, it may not appear to be so on the surface. Shamans see the life force behind the outer manifestation and are capable of communicating with it.

To understand your power animal you first need to identify it. We have a wide range of methods to do this. Many native people, including North American Indians and the Inuit, traditionally went out on a three- or four-day vision quest to spend time alone in nature, fasting and praying for the animal to reveal itself.

Finding your spirit animal using various dreaming methods is another time-tested technique, very powerful because it makes direct contact with the animal spirit. The drum journey is another effective method. Some of these methods will be described here, so that you have different options, and I recommend you begin with the one that appeals to you the most.

✦ DREAMING ✦

In a dream state, the mind, which has been in charge of our consciousness during the day, is no longer in control. As soon as we fall asleep the mind lets go, our awareness deepens, and our consciousness enters another realm—that of the soul and spirit. This is a world of images, metaphors, symbols, and, according to the shamanic tradition, spirit contact.

In a dream state we are free, we can fly, and we can experience and learn things that would be impossible in our waking life. In our dreams we can meet our ancestors, our spirit teachers, and our power animals.

Shamans work with an understanding of the dream state, and they have given us ways to begin to enter the dream realm more consciously and experience its gifts. This is sometimes referred to as the art of dreaming.

Dreaming, or "vision quest," rather than a drum journey, was the traditional way in which native people sought their spirit animals. Often dreams and visions were considered to be the same, and many native cultures do not differentiate linguistically between the two experiences. In this book, when I use the term "dreaming" in relation to the methods and exercises, I usually refer to the dreaming that happens while you are asleep.

When you dream, you usually have little or no influence as to what you experience. However, when you embark on a 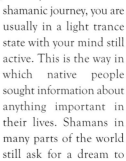 shamanic journey, you are usually in a light trance state with your mind still active. This is the way in which native people sought information about anything important in their lives. Shamans in many parts of the world still ask for a dream to show them how to treat a patient. In the dream they might be shown a particular herb, which they then find and pick the following day. By asking for something to be revealed to you in a dream, you are surrendering on a deep level and trusting that what comes to you does so from a spirit source. Today, this way of working is frequently called "dream induction."

Dream induction can be practiced by anyone almost straight away, but it is useful to learn some basic dreaming skills if you want to work with your dreams and become more proficient. Dreaming is an amazing method for gaining self-understanding and connecting with spiritual dimensions. All dream work begins with good dream recall.

Dream recall

We dream every night, and have many more dreams than we remember. Recall is a way to begin to bring more and more dreams into your waking awareness. It is a little like throwing out a fishing line and pulling the fish into shore one by one. Here the fish are your dreams, the line is your pen and journal, and the shore is your waking consciousness.

To develop dream recall skills, keep a journal in which you write your dreams every morning. Practice being very still and quiet when you wake to catch your dreams before they disappear. If you wake in the night from a dream, write it in your journal straight away rather than assume you will remember it in the morning; it will likely be lost. When you have kept a journal for a while, you will find that this in itself begins to awaken your ability to interpret your dreams. You will also find that, when you look back at dreams, what initially you didn't understand begins to make a lot of sense. For many people, keeping a dream journal helps profoundly with a process of self-understanding and the realization of their potential.

A clear mind

While you are sleeping at night your mind begins to revisit all your experiences of the day, or even your lifetime, which your consciousness has not fully integrated. Much night-time energy is spent clearing what has been left unresolved so

Writing a Dream Journal

1 Keep a pen and a dream journal at your bedside. Put a flashlight there as well if you sleep with anyone else, to avoid waking them up by turning on a light.

2 Always write your dreams down straight after waking, even if it is in the middle of the night.

3 Read your dream journal occasionally to learn about yourself and your power animal.

Reviewing the Day

1 In the evening, before you lie down in bed, go over the day in your mind. Look at everything you have done and, as far as possible, come to terms with what has happened and complete unfinished aspects of your experience. In this way you free up energy for dreaming.

2 To fall asleep with a clear mind and in a high state of consciousness, meditate or focus on your breath for a few minutes so that you feel peaceful.

Practicing the Well

1 Before you fall asleep at night, imagine yourself sitting by a well.

2 Visualize yourself writing the following on a piece of paper: "I (your full name) will remember my dreams when I wake up in the morning." Sign the paper.

3 Imagine yourself folding the paper many times, then let it drop into the well. Visualize your folded message sinking all the way to the bottom of the well.

4 Now you can go to sleep.

you can wake up in as focused a state of mind as possible.

Dealing with unresolved issues from the day while you sleep takes time and energy, affecting how deeply you sleep as well as your dreams. The more you have already cleared issues from your psyche before you go to sleep, the more energy you have free for medicine dreams. This is why many native people, and shamans in particular, review the day before they go to sleep. It is also vital to get enough sleep as doing so enables your mind to recall dreams more clearly.

The well

When I first began to work with animal spirits in shamanism, I learnt a very effec-

tive method called "The Well," which promotes dream recall. I have taught it frequently and received many positive responses from those who have used it. This method programs your mind at a deep level to be able to recall your dreams on awakening.

Diet and dream recall

Your brain needs certain chemicals to allow it to remember dreams. While there are many theories about how "brain food" links to dream recall, it does seem clear that B6 vitamins and lecithin, a soya product, help the brain to retain the information given in dreams. However, do seek professional advice if you plan to take supplements.

Dream induction

Dream induction is the classical shamanic method of seeking spiritual guidance, and a good way to meet your spirit animal. It has been practiced around the world through the ages—in Ancient Greece, for example, temples were built for the specific purpose of dream induction.

The power of your intention as well as your trust is required to work in this way. Prayer is also useful in your work with animal spirits. Keep in mind that animal spirits are beings with their own free will; when you call on them and they come to you, they offer the gift of their presence. Gratitude and giving thanks are therefore appropriate, and are things you can give in return to strengthen the bond between you.

Dream induction involves posing a question before you fall asleep and asking for the answer to come to you while you are in the dream state. When the question centers on discovering your power animal, you may have to ask the question many times, or you may receive the answer straight away. You have two options—asking repeatedly until the answer comes, or asking occasionally. On the nights of a dream induction, prepare yourself during the day by thinking about your question and summoning positive energy within yourself. This paves the way for an answer to come through a dream.

Calling your Power Animal into a Dream

Here is one way of using dream induction to find your power animal:

1 When you are in bed and ready to sleep, state your intention in your own words. For example: "I will meet my power animal in my dreams tonight. Power animal, please reveal yourself to me in my dreams tonight!" State your intention several times. Call on the highest power to protect you.

2 Relax and enter a state of trusting that whatever is supposed to happen will happen, and that it will be right, whatever it is. Let yourself fall asleep.

3 Keep a pen and dream journal at your bedside and write your dreams down as soon as you wake up.

Intention

Most importantly for dream induction is to have a strong intention that you will receive an answer in your dreams. This kind of intention is a blend of willing the dream to arrive and detaching your mind from trying to control what happens. This is something of a paradox, but vital. If you use only willpower, repeatedly pushing for a result, you will be trying to force an answer. However, the relaxed approach alone—

simply trusting and doing nothing—may not work either. The best way is to merge elements of both, by building intention.

Building intention during the day

In the waking hours of your day, think about your intention and repeat it to yourself—for example, you might repeat the statement that you will meet your spirit animal in your dreams.

Repeat this regularly during the day, making your intention as strong as possible so that it carries over into your dreams. You can even use a reminder such as a bracelet or a finger ring that you wear solely for this purpose, so that every time you look at it you are reminded of your intention.

Practicing Building Intention

1 In the morning, decide your intention for your dreams during the night to come.

2 Remind yourself of your intention several times throughout the day, building the intention.

3 You can use a reminder such as a bracelet, a finger ring, or set a wrist watch to beep every hour, taking you back to your intention.

4 Repeat the intention before falling asleep.

Working with your Third Eye

1 Take a nap during the day lying on your back, and set a strong intention to meet your power animal.

2 Your daytime nap can last between five minutes and half an hour. The images you see in this state are sometimes hypnogogic, and tend to flood your mind just before the state of sleep begins.

Naps, or transition states

When you go to sleep there is a transition time between the waking and sleeping state. During this time, you have the potential to experience a phenomenon that shamans and other seers have worked with since ancient times: hypnogogic imagery. This is experienced in the form of images flooding your inner eye. The inner eye (or the third eye, or shamanic eye) is one of the body's 12 energy centers, or chakras.

You can work with these images, which tend to appear just before sleep, using shamanic techniques that connect us with the spiritual realms and our power animal. It is important to enter this process without trying to influence the discovery of your power animal by forcing thoughts of the one you want to see.

✦ THE DRUM JOURNEY ✦

To understand the drum journey, it is helpful to think about the Cosmos as it was—and is—perceived by many native people around the globe.

Cosmos is seen to be like a big tree, called The Tree Of Life. The crown is the Upper World, the trunk represents the Middle World, and the roots represent the Lower World.

Humans live in the Middle World. This is physical reality as we know it, the place where we spend our time from birth until death, and where we experience everything with our physical senses and our rational mind. If you only perceive with your mind, it is easy to think that only this realm exists.

The Upper World is the realm of spirit teachers, illuminated masters and ancestors. Sometimes referred to as Heaven, the upper world, as experienced by native people in shamanic practice, is a complex realm with many different dimensions.

Power animals, as well as some of our ancestors, occupy the Lower World. This is a world of strong grounding and healing energies, and is the place to go when you need such qualities and powers.

Drum journeys are not only a good way to find your power animal, but a means to stay connected with it. Used widely among many native cultures, the monotonous, fast beat of the drum induces a trance that enables us to alter our consciousness. We can then perceive on a spiritual level rather than the rational, physical realm our mind usually occupies in everyday life.

You can ask someone to drum for you while you go on your spiritual journey, but if this is not possible then a CD with a shamanic drum beat—a journey beat—will work. A typical journey beat is between 200 and 230 beats per minute.

Embarking on a drum journey is a ceremony in itself. To make it as effective, reliable, and safe as possible, begin by preparing yourself and the place you will be working in. Avoid alcohol and drugs and eat only lightly before the journey so that your mind is clear and alert. Make sure you will not be disturbed.

Begin by calling on the power of the seven directions, which consist of the sky, the earth, the four cardinal points, and the center. Draw an invisible circle around yourself to create a safe area. Light a

Opposite: In shamanic cultures the Cosmos is perceived as The Tree of Life, which has three realms of existence: The Middle World, the Upper World, and the Lower World.

candle, the sacred fire, and call on the highest powers to be present and to guide you as you journey. The more intention and sincerity that you put into the preparation, the more effective it is likely to be. You are not only creating a safe space but a spiritual one.

Once you feel you have established your sacred space, start the drumming. Sit, in a meditation posture, with your eyes covered, maybe with a headscarf or bandana, to keep out the light. You can also lie down if you prefer. Visualize an opening in the earth. Choose a place already familiar to you, such as a cave you have visited, a foxhole, or a hole between the roots of a tree that you have seen while out walking. Visualize yourself standing at this opening into the earth. See your free soul, your double—the part of you that can journey out of your body when you are dreaming—standing in front of the hole. Now begin to journey down the hole and through a tunnel. Soon you will enter a beautiful landscape of pure unspoiled nature—mountains, rivers, and plains—the realm of animal spirits, the Lower World.

When you reach the Lower World remind yourself of the purpose of your journey—to find your power animal. Your mission is literally to seek it and there are different ways to identify it. If an animal comes to you, you can ask it directly whether it is your power animal. It will respond positively if it is, but in any case your heart will usually know whether it is your power animal or not—a deep, inner sense will tell you. In some traditions, shamans say that if the animal you meet shows itself from all sides, then it is your power animal.

Make contact with your power animal and tell it that you want to stay connected with it. Thank it before returning through the tunnel, then up through the hole, exactly the way you came.

When you get up from your meditative position it can be a good idea to invite your power animal to dance through you. This means it guides you in how to dance. The dance does not need to be elaborate or wild; you might simply move around, letting into your body the sensation—usually a charge of energy—from your power animal. The dance confirms and strengthens the connection between you.

After your journey and the dance, give thanks to the powers that have assisted you. It is then important to ground yourself and return fully into your body. To ground yourself effectively, stretch gently, breath deeply, or eat a snack.

Embarking on a Drum Journey

Here is a step-by-step guide to undertaking a drum journey:

1 Call on the power of the seven directions—sky, earth, east, south, west, north, and center—in your own words. Call on the highest power to protect you. Create a sacred space by drawing an invisible circle around you and lighting a candle.

2 Sit down on a chair or on the floor, or lie down on your back on a blanket, in a darkened room and make yourself comfortable. Close your eyes and take some deep breaths. Focus on the rhythm of your breathing, and let it bring you into a relaxed state of mind.

3 Turn on the drumming CD. Cover your eyes with a bandana or scarf, and imagine yourself standing in front of a hole that leads into the ground, for instance a hole at the foot of a tree, or a cave. Any natural opening that leads into the earth will do. Imagine yourself going through the opening and descending along a tunnel into the land of the power animals. You will come to a beautiful, untouched wilderness with meadows, mountains, rivers, and trees.

4 Call on your power animal and ask it to reveal itself. If more than one animal appears, then ask which one is your power animal—usually your heart will know.

5 Thank your power animal, and tell it you want to stay connected with it. Return to your physical body, traveling back the way you came through the tunnel and hole in the earth.

6 Invite your power animal to dance with you. Feel yourself merge with it and experience its power.

7 Give thanks to the powers of the seven directions and dissolve your circle. Extinguish the candle.

8 Bring your awareness back into your body by stretching, doing some physical activity, or eating something. Make sure you are fully grounded before you go out into the world.

CHAPTER TWO

WORKING WITH YOUR POWER ANIMAL

✦ AUTHENTICITY ✦

By starting to work with your power animal, you enter a process of finding your true strength. The most evident lesson gleaned from animal spirits is that of authenticity. This is at the core of animal spirit teachings. Power animals, if you invite them to do so, have the capacity to awaken within you the deep authenticity that they possess within themselves. They are without pretence, and they can show you the way to find this genuine state within yourself.

Authenticity is more important than power, and it is free from moral judgment. When a hawk kills a blackbird, the act is neither good nor bad. The hawk kills the little bird in order to eat. It doesn't make much sense to say: "I like the hawk, but I don't like the fact that it kills blackbirds." We need to accept both the grace of the hawk and that it kills as part of the natural order. It is hard to truly choose before we have first accepted all that is part of life. If you only focus on what you want to see,

Bringing Gifts

Native people often have a concept of living in a harmonious relationship with all that exists. Through understanding this concept, you can learn to live in balance with yourself and with everything that is around you. It is appropriate to give something to your power animal in return for answering your request. The animal spirit has no obligation to come, so expressing your gratitude honors its free will, and demonstrates that you come from a place of respect.

Traditionally, people gave offerings to their animal spirits in the form of food, herbs, and incense. However, simply saying "thank you" to your animals is sufficient. Future contact becomes easier when you have given something in return for the gift of your animal spirit's presence, and it helps to strengthen the bond between you.

blocking out what is distasteful to you, your choices may not be based on reality, since you have deliberately limited your field of vision.

Human beings have tools of intellect and reflection, which are great powers. However, without balance, they can cause you to lose your way in the maze of your mind, so that you lose your authentic self. Think what a relief it is to be in the company of people who are just being themselves. This is one way in which power animals have tremendous gifts for us: authenticity and a non-judgmental approach. We can learn from our power animals and become more like them.

✦ COMPASSION ✦

Why would animal spirits have anything to do with humans, considering the way in which we treat the Earth, animals, and each other?

The teachings in this subject can often take time to comprehend. Traditionally, insight amongst shamans has revealed a common belief that animal spirits are under guidance from higher spirit beings—immediately from the collective spirit of their animal species, and ultimately from the highest power of the divine. Behind the animal spirits that help us, therefore, is the highest power. Animals are in service to such powers, and this service is seen as part of their evolution on the level of soul.

On this soul level, most animals have what we would term as "compassion" for human beings, and that is why animal spirits are willing to work with us. The sacred trust between animals and humans is based on compassion. It is what makes cooperation possible.

We humans experience a compassion that tends to be sentimental in its nature. The compassion shown by animals, being non-sentimental, is true compassion. As human beings, we should practice non-sentimental compassion in our relations with animals. Working with your power animal might inspire you to think about what you can do for animals in general, and to make a commitment to doing it.

✦ THE BRIDGE ✦

Once you have found your power animal you can begin to look for an object that will work as a bridge between you. It can be anything: a wood or stone carving in the shape of that animal, or a stone with the animal painted on it. If possible, it could also be a part of that animal such as a piece of fur, a tooth, or a claw. The object will help make the connection between you stronger, and it will begin to hold power in itself and become what is called a "power object." This means that some of the animal spirit's energy has been transferred into the item. You can encourage this transmission of power by holding the object in your hands while you do a med-itation: call on your power animal, asking it to awaken the object and imbue it with some of the animal's own power. From then on, it is important to care properly for the object because it is now truly alive. This means cleansing it regularly in running water so that you wash away unwanted energies it may have accumulated. For cleansing purposes, you can also use incense and herbs such as sage, lavender, or rosemary.

Keep the object in your pocket or put it into a small pouch hung on a string around your neck. Whenever you want to contact your power animal, take hold of the object.

Keeping a Power Object

1 Find an appropriate item to help you connect with your power animal.

2 Hold the object in your hands and call on your power animal. Ask it to awaken the object and to transfer some of its own power into the object.

3 Keep the object in your pocket or put it in a pouch that you hang around your neck so that it is close to your heart.

4 Hold the pouch when you want to contact your power animal.

5 Cleanse the power object regularly in running water or with incense or herbs.

Studying Your Power
Animals, or Hunting
Your Self

When you have found your power animal, study it to become more familiar with its personality, its habitat, its diet, and everything else about it (see Chapter Four). You can make this kind of study through reading, watching wildlife footage, or, ideally, by observing it in nature. As well as being your guardian, your power animal is a reflection of your soul and personality, so studying it will give you many personal insights.

When I began shamanic work 25 years ago, my teacher recommended that I start hunting myself with the goal of gathering knowledge on all levels, and so begin a long journey of self-discovery. All major spiritual traditions recognize that this needs to be a corner stone in spiritual development. Hunter-animals, such as mountain lions and jaguars, are excellent teachers of this art.

You will begin to learn about your own strengths and weaknesses by looking at those of your power animal. For example, eagle flies high and has a broad perspective

of things from above, which is a great gift and strength. However, that gift has a shadow side because the eagle may also have a tendency to feel isolated and superior to the rest of creation. The eagle therefore needs to learn to be grounded, to come down to the earth and be in close contact with it, like mouse. By contrast, mouse's power is that she is in close proximity to everything she sees, studying it in detail and discovering through touch. She then needs to learn to gain a wider perspective on life.

We should not make our power animal an excuse for certain kinds of behavior detrimental to us or to other people. Let's say your animal is jaguar, and you tend to isolate yourself from others. The behavior of jaguar, who lives alone most of the time, should not be an excuse for you to remain isolated. You are not a jaguar, you are a human being who needs to be socially involved with others, even while you carry the traits of jaguar.

Journey to your Power Animal

You can use the drum journey to contact your power animal so as to ask it questions, seek help with a specific issue, or just to stay connected with it. The first step is to find out exactly what it is you need and the second step is to inform your power animal. The more specific you can be in clarifying what you need before you begin the communication, the more effective it will usually be.

The drum journey described in Chapter One is basically the same technique used here, except that now you already know your power animal, and your mission has changed to the search for an answer to your question.

Asking for Help

1 Call on the power of the seven directions—sky, earth, east, south, west, north, and center. Draw the invisible circle around you and light a candle. Ask the highest power for to protect you.

2 Sit down on a chair or on the floor, or lie down on your back on a blanket in a darkened room, making yourself comfortable. Close your eyes and take some deep breaths. Focus on the rhythm of your breathing, and let it bring you into a relaxed state of mind.

3 Turn on the drumming CD. Cover your eyes with a bandana or scarf, and imagine yourself standing in front of a hole that leads into the ground. Any natural opening that leads into the earth—for example, a hole at the foot of a tree, or a cave—will

do. Imagine yourself going through the opening and descending along a tunnel into the land of the power animals. You will come to a beautiful, untouched wilderness with meadows, mountains, rivers, and trees.

4 Call on your animal spirit and ask it to reveal itself. Tell it why you have come and ask it the question you bring.

5 Thank your power animal. Return to your physical body, traveling back the way you came.

6 Give thanks to the powers of the seven directions and dissolve your circle. Extinguish the candle.

7 Bring your awareness back into your body by stretching, doing some physical activity, or eating.

✦ COMPANIONSHIP ✦

You can call upon your power animal in many different situations. One might be when you need extra strength; if you connect with your power animal before an interview, for example, you can ask it for support. Sense how your power animal would enter the room, and how it would be centered. Feel its dignity, its realness, and courage within you. Now your personal power can be expressed with clarity.

As we have seen, learning about a power animal is very much about learning to build an authentic self. This means letting go of the pretences we have often grafted onto our personality. When as children we learn to fit in socially, we often "wear" attributes other than our own. If we continue in this way we eventually follow a path of false identity. Your power animal can help bring you home to yourself.

Looking at old photographic prints of the native peoples of Siberia, North and South America, and the Sami people of Scandinavia, it is noticeable that at times the people and their power animals merge; you can see the strong qualities of animals in their faces. Our life today is obviously different from that depicted in such images

and, unlike those people, we do not need to merge with our power animals to such an extent. Although we too are engaged in the evolution of our souls, we do not live so closely with nature. A high degree of merging with animal spirits is no longer necessary for our physical survival, though they still have an important role in our soul evolution.

Make your power animal a true friend and companion, and let there be equality between you. Never hand over your self-authority. This means avoiding any situation in which you might do something you do not feel is right, then justify your action by telling yourself that your power animal was in charge. You are in charge, and you make your own decisions. At the same time, develop the skills of your power animal since animal spirits have qualities that are superior to ours. These include grounding, clarity, alertness, compassion, positivity, knowing the right action to take in any situation, and an acute sense of direction (see the animal spirit guides in Chapter Four). Power animals are willing to teach us how to connect with all the qualities latent in our potential as individuals.

DREAMING WITH YOUR POWER ANIMAL

In the shamanic tradition a visitation from a power animal in a dream is usually seen as a blessing and a gift. During the encounter, a transfer of energy often takes place. The power animal may give you strength, insight, clarity, and hope. People generally wake with an uplifted feeling after these encounters.

Your work with a power animal can continue in the dreamtime, so that dreaming becomes a way of staying connected. Using the following method (see also the summary on page 42), which is similar to the dream induction for finding your power animal described in Chapter One, you can begin to interact with your power animal. You will now need more awareness in the dream state and a stronger intention.

Before going to bed at night, begin by clearing your space energetically. The objective here is to create an internal state and an external atmosphere conducive to contact with animal spirits. You can do this by burning incense or herbs to cleanse the area around you. Spirit helpers also like the sweet fragrances released from burning herbs or grasses, and this encourages them to be near you. The process of clearing a room, an object, or a person with the smoke from burning herbs is called smudging, and is practiced by most spiritual traditions and religions.

The next step is to call on the highest power or Great Spirit using whatever name you are comfortable with, and ask that you will be blessed and protected in your sleep and dreams. By doing so you also set a high standard for yourself, and state an intention to work in higher spiritual realms. In the dream state your intention can take you to these benevolent and healing realms, or to lower emotional and energetic domains, just as in waking life.

Review your day to clear your mind as described in Chapter One (page 25). Your purpose is to be in as clear a state as possible before sleep so that your mind will not need to spend so much time processing unfinished business from the day.

Focus on your breathing for a couple of minutes, then do a meditation in which you meet your power animal and invite it

Opposite: You can ask a higher power to take you to a realm of healing and connection in which you can meet your power animal and ask for inspiration and support.

Welcoming Your Power Animal into Dreams

1 Cleanse your space using incense or herbs with the intention of creating an atmosphere conducive for contact with your power animal.

2 Call on the highest power using whatever name you are comfortable with and ask for blessings and protection.

3 Clear your mind using the method in Chapter One called "Reviewing the Day" (page 25).

4 Focus on your breathing for a couple of minutes before visiting your power animal and asking it to come into your dreams.

5 See in your mind's eye that you meet your power animal in your dreams. State your intention for the dream meeting and see yourself telling your power animal what you seek from the meeting. Make the intention very strong.

6 Fall asleep in a state of trust, having let go of attachments to your day, in particular any worries. Fall asleep in a state of peace.

to come into your dreams (see above). Build a strong intention that this will happen, visualizing yourself meeting your power animal this way. State your intention for the dream meeting. Maybe you want to ask your power animal a question,

ask it to take you to a certain location, or help with a problem. Or your incentive might just be to spend time together.

At last, you let go and surrender into trust that whatever happens will be right. Let go of any attachments and fall asleep.

✦ ANIMAL SPIRIT HELPERS ✦

Your power animal is your main guardian and a mirror of your personality—it can also be termed your soul animal, because on a soul level you are one. This animal spirit will usually stay with you for your entire life. For specific tasks or projects, however, you may want the assistance of other animal spirit helpers.

Let's say your power animal is an owl and that your profession is to work with sports injuries—as a sports massage therapist, for example. The owl is your guardian spirit and you will resemble owl in numerous ways, but you might also have an animal spirit helper who comes to assist you in your work. Bear's medicine is healing, so perhaps she might channel some healing energy through your hands. Another example might be someone who

has mountain lion as a power animal and is a soccer coach for children in his spare time. Otter might be an animal spirit helper who brings some play and fun into his coaching.

Sometimes such helpers come of their own accord and will assist even without their beneficiaries being aware of them, working invisibly in parallel. You can also actively seek an animal spirit helper for a specific purpose, traveling to find the appropriate helper and requesting assistance. Remember that if you journey seeking a specific animal, you may not find it. Animal spirits have free will, and usually choose us, rather than us choosing them. When they come to help you with a specific task they will usually stay for a while, then leave once the job is done.

Contacting an Animal Spirit Helper

1 Identify a specific area in your life where you need help. It can be anything: emotional, spiritual, practical, professional.

2 Undertake a shamanic journey to find an animal helper different from your power animal, using the Drum Journey method described in Chapter One (pages 26–29).

3 Ask for specific instructions or teachings from the new animal spirit.

CHAPTER THREE

THE WAYS OF THE SHAMAN

✦ Making it Genuine ✦

People who come to my introductory workshops often ask, when we begin to contact power animals: "How do I know I'm not making this up?" And, "How do I know my mind is not making up that my power animal is a stag because I don't want it to be a mouse?" Or, "How can I be sure that I'm really meeting this power animal, and not creating it all in my mind?"

Those are good questions; the mind is constantly making things up because it wants to be in control and feel that it has an answer to everything. However, no matter how wonderful a tool it is, we don't meet spirit helpers by means of our rational mind. We use our heart and spirit. The answer to the question is that your heart knows, and will tell you if it is true and real.

We need to trust and continue to practice developing genuine spirit contact. In my experience dreaming is reliable, because your rational mind is not in control any longer. In meditations and journeys part of your awareness is still in your physical body, but this is not the case when you dream. If you develop your dreaming skills, as most of my native teachers emphasized, then you have a reliable spiritual tool.

There are further ways to deepen your work, to make your spirit contact more real and to bring it out of the realm of mind games. In this chapter I describe how to work with your power animal using energy lines. This method takes practice, but it will help bring your connection with your power animal to a new level—and you will have no more doubts about whether or not it is real.

✦ THE SHAMAN'S CORD ✦

Traditionally, indigenous shamans have used energy lines when working with power animals. One method—the shaman's cord—involves using your energy centers, or chakras (see also the exercise summary overleaf). For the cord method, the most important energy center is the will, (also known as *hara* in Japan).

The will is located just below your navel and is an internal center of life force and gravity. It is from this center that you will send out an energetic line, or cord. You can back up the power of the will center with your base center, which is located at the base of the spine.

For the cord method you will also use the shamanic eye, also known as the third eye, which is located just above and between the physical eyes, for perceiving your power animal. From your heart center you will invite the power animal to come and work with you. The other chakras, or energy centers, of the body can be used as well, but these four—the base, will, heart, and shamanic eye—are the most important for the cord method.

Activating your energy centers

Firstly, create a sacred area to work in. Smudge the room and yourself, burn some dried herbs or incense, and light a candle. Call on the seven directions as described in The Drum Journey in Chapter One (pages 26–29), for protection and to define your ceremonial space, and ask the highest power to oversee your ceremony.

You are now ready to activate your energy centers. This must be done in a strong way for the rest of the ceremony to work. You can activate your energy centers by breathing deeply into them. Drumming, such as by playing a drum journey CD, or singing can also help to activate energy centers. When you feel your centers are activated, call on the animal spirit to come and be in front of you. Send out a line, or energy cord, from your will center to the animal spirit. From your heart invite it to come and merge with you, and perceive it from your third eye. Invite your power animal to travel to you on the energy cord you have sent out toward it. When the animal spirit reaches your body, let it merge with you. In order for this to happen, your energy centers need to be completely active.

When the animal has merged with you, ask it to help awaken a quality inside yourself that you are ready to engage with. This might be a quality that the animal already possesses, but it could be any quality. If the animal spirit is wild boar, for example, it might help you awaken courage. Ask that the quality be activated on a cellular level.

Once you feel that the power of this quality is within you, thank the animal spirit and the powers of the seven directions for supporting you, and dissolve the protective circle they have helped to create around you. Extinguish the candle. The ceremony is then complete.

This method can be used for many different purposes. You can also repeat it several times for one specific purpose, such as the one mentioned here, until you feel the quality you need is truly awakened.

With this way of working you have a genuine experience of interlinking your consciousness with that of the animal spirit, and sometimes it is as if you become one and experience true union. The way of the shaman is very much about union—stepping out of the illusion of separation and experiencing oneness.

Using the Cord Method

1 Create a sacred space. Smudge and call on the seven directions to create a circle around you. Light a candle. Ask the highest power for protection.

2 Activate your energy centers using breathing, drumming, possibly a drum journey CD, and singing if it helps you.

3 Call on the animal spirit. Send out an energy cord from your will center and invite the animal spirit to travel along the cord and merge with you. Ask it to activate the quality that you are ready to manifest.

4 Thank the animal spirit and let it return. Thank the powers of the four directions and dissolve your circle. Extinguish the candle.

✦ SHAPE SHIFTING ✦

Traditionally, shamans carry out the art of shape shifting to become their power animal, being in two places at the same time—something we have probably all wished we could do!

Shape shifting and existing in two places at the same time are not metaphors, however, but a physical transformation that many shamans have mastered. This phenomenon was universal, regardless of the separation between continents, and it has been perceived and experienced by native peoples all over the Earth in very much the same way.

Shamans perceive spiritual reality through the highly developed faculties of clairvoyance (visual), clairsentience (feeling), clairaudience (hearing), and claircognizance (mind), then make their experiences known to others.

Shape shifting allows shamans to travel in the form of their power animal, visiting other places to explore, to heal, or just for the sheer joy of it. It is a highly advanced skill, and only a few people on the planet today are capable of it.

However, there is a way to have this experience in dreamtime. Shape shifting when you are dreaming feels real, as if you are having the actual experience. It offers you an amazing, mind-blowing feeling of freedom when you fly in the body of a falcon or gallop as a horse across wild plains.

Union is a state in which you can experience ecstasy. When you have merged with your power animal, the union of consciousness can be ecstatic; shamanism is sometimes referred to as "the art of ecstasy."

When you have learned to shape shift in the dream state, you will know the reason why. Your sense of reality expands, and you realize that your physical body alone does not constitute what you are. You are much more than that, and you can merge with the body of an animal and still retain the essence of your own self. This "shift" state reveals something about illusions, and the illusive nature of reality as we normally define it.

Shape shifting while dreaming

Dreaming is a reliable method for contacting your power animal, and it can lead to the out-of-body experience I consider to be the next step after learning meditations and drum journeys.

To develop your grasp of this method, meditate before you go to bed at night, building your intention in order to program your consciousness toward your objective. Again, you first need to smudge the room and yourself. Then follow the method for Reviewing the Day in Chapter One to go through the day and clear your feelings so that your energy is not sapped and your mind does not need to process what has happened (see page 25). Instead, it is free to dream.

The first step toward being able to shape shift into your power animal while asleep is to become aware that you are dreaming. Now referred to as lucid dreaming, this is an ancient skill of the shaman and other spiritual institutions—one of my teachers on dreaming was a lama from the Tibetan tradition. Although there are many different ways in which to recognize consciously that you are dreaming, this is the method that I personally use most of the time: When going to bed in the evening, enter a meditation in which you seek grounding, allowing your mind and

Right: Centering and calming the mind with meditation and setting an intention before sleep can help bring about a shape-shifting experience.

body to become one, and being firmly in your center. If you carry this feeling into sleep, you will find that it helps you to identify the dream state.

Recognizing the dream state

Make a strong intention that you will recognize you are dreaming. State the intention that you will be aware of anything that appears different from ordinary reality. This could be a bodily sensation, such as being too heavy to run or feeling so light that you can take off from the ground. Notice if people behave differently than how they would normally behave. Question anything unusual and ask yourself if you are dreaming.

You need to have a clear plan for what you will do once you have realized that you are dreaming. Say to yourself: "Next time I dreaming, I will remember to shape shift into my power animal."

What is your intention when you have shape shifted? If you are a falcon, maybe there will be a certain destination you can fly to, experiencing falcon's razor-sharp vision. If you are a deer perhaps you will be running through the woods, learning about how it feels for deer to do that— noticing the animal's acute sense of smell and hearing.

Sometimes it can be a delicate balance to stay in the body of the power animal.

Learning to Shape Shift

1 Smudge your room and yourself.

2 Go over the day to clear your mind.

3 Center and ground yourself in a meditation. Ask the highest power for protection.

4 State your intention to recognize that you are dreaming by noticing anything unusual while in the dream state.

5 Affirm your intention to shape shift into your power animal. Do this several times, investing a lot of power into the statement.

6 Let go and surrender into trust. Let yourself fall asleep.

If your awareness starts to drift you can lose the contact easily and glide back into unconscious dreaming. Although at other times you might stay focused, it is good to prepare by keeping as clear an intention as possible so as to remain lucid.

This experience, in which there is unity and blending of consciousness, helps to create a powerful bond between you and your power animal. The animal spirit also becomes so real for you that a door to new adventures opens and the possibilities are endless.

SIGNS:
MESSAGES FROM SPIRIT

Closely related to the teachings on power animals is the ability to read and understand signs. Signs are messages from the higher, spiritual realms sent to guide you, teach you, or even to warn you. Appearing at appropriate times, they may be strong and unmistakable, or easy to dismiss. Shamans have always been aware of signs and omens, including those brought by animals. Signs are directly linked to the teaching on The Magical Mirror (page 8).

When you connect with your power animal you link not only with the individual spirit of your power animal, but also with the collective spirit, or consciousness, of its species. Each group of animals has this collective spirit. For example, imagine that you are walking through fields, perhaps bordered by trees. Maybe you stop for a moment to take in the landscape. You are thinking about whether or not to apply for a job you have heard is available. Suddenly a hawk flies down and catches a mouse close to you. A shaman would say that you were given a clear sign to go for it and that, because the hawk got the mouse, you would probably be successful too. If, on the other hand, the hawk had not caught the mouse, the sign would tell

you that you could apply for the job, but you might not get it.

We can look further into such signs by noticing the direction an animal comes from and returns to when it appears to us. In the hawk and mouse scenario, should the hawk that had missed the mouse fly away toward the east, then it may be in that geographical direction that another job for you is located. Let your heart guide you to understand the signs.

The hawk giving the sign has moved from its own individual consciousness into the collective consciousness of all hawks. This collective consciousness links with the web of all life, where nothing is hidden. The hawk knows exactly what you need at that moment. However, according to my teacher, there is divine energy behind the hawk, because the spirit of all hawks is directly connected to the divine. We can read the sequence like this:

Hawk—Spirit Of All Hawks—the Divine.

Opposite: Looking at the natural world and understanding the connection between the lower, middle, and higher realms of existence helps us link with signs from our animal spirit guides.

As you have seen, this principle also applies to your power animal. Understanding the link helps us to see how power animals can be so illuminated. When you receive a sign, remember that it comes ultimately from the divine and give your thanks.

However, as every sighting of an animal does not mean receiving a sign, how can we tell the difference? Firstly, by being grounded and using common sense. Remember not to give away your self-authority. No matter how many great signs you receive, you are still the one in charge, and you make your own decisions. Practice the balance between free will and guidance from spirit. Your heart—not your mind or your emotions—will be able to tell you what is right. Many people equate emotions with the heart, but in the medicine tradition I was taught, they are different. Emotions are linked to the solar plexus center, which shamans call the power center. In this tradition, emotions are related both to power and danger. They can be powerful and nourish us, but they can also be extremely dangerous, resulting in conflict or even war. The heart is a place of higher feelings such as compassion and love, and it is the seat of deep inner knowing about what is right and wrong. This is why we talk about the clarity of the heart.

As well as signs, you may receive confirmations, or agreements. If you are sitting in a cafe talking with friends and you say: "Maybe I should consider stopping smoking," and immediately the words have left your mouth a dog barks outside, then I would call that a confirmation. It is the universe agreeing with what you have said. Although not necessarily a great medicine sign, it should still be taken seriously.

Medicine walks

There are ways to seek out medicine signs. This is particularly appropriate if you have an important question that you need an answer to, or if you need guidance to make a choice. As an alternative, or maybe in addition, to a drum journey or asking for a dream, you can take a medicine walk.

Set aside a period of time, from 15 minutes up to a whole day or even longer. Firstly, formulate and state your question, then ask Mother Earth for guidance on your walk. Set out on your walk alone and choose an area where you do not need to interact with other people. Let go of all other thoughts and pay attention to what is going on around you. Walking in nature, it is easy to enter an altered state of consciousness. Although this is the traditional way to experience a medicine walk, I have heard of good results from groups of people I have sent on medicine walks in cities such as Amsterdam when I have taught workshops there. This goes to show that this work can be done wherever you are. The mirror is everywhere, and Mother Earth is always here to teach us.

As you walk attentively, what happens around you can inform you about the question you hold, just as in a dream. If you see ducks in a pond making noise and seeming to enjoy themselves, perhaps that is what you need to learn to do, and perhaps it answers part of your question. It is not only animals that bring you signs. They can also come in other forms such as a jet plane flying overhead, a passing bicycle or, if you are in a city, a conversation you overhear as a family walks past you in the street.

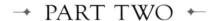

PART TWO

ANIMAL SPIRIT GUIDES

In this chapter you will find a description of
more than 60 different animals and their medicine.
In most cases I give an account of the real-life meeting I
have had with the animal and what I have observed. For
others, I used the dreaming method, and in some cases the
drum journey, described in this book, to meet the animals and
experience their qualities, habitats, and teachings. Dreaming is,
in some ways, close to real-life experience, and the dream
encounters with a number of these animals not only opened
my understanding of them, but established a
bond between us.

ANIMAL SPIRITS
✦ AND THE ELEMENTS ✦

For ease of reference the animals described here have been grouped according to their habitat, rather than the essence and quality of the elemental forces within each of them. The four groups are earth, air, water, and water/earth.

The groups in their correlation with the elements each hold certain qualities, described in the following pages. These qualities are present within each of us, as well as in the animals written about here. When looking to understand the medicine of an animal, we must also study the element(s) in which it is at home.

The element fire is not used as a grouping, but in the description of the animals you will find that fire is present as an inner quality amongst many of them. In this way, all four elemental powers are represented.

Fire, water, earth, and air are spiritual powers infused with consciousness. They play a central role in the spiritual teachings of native people. They can be communicated with and meditated on, and if we begin to do so we can understand why they play such a key role for native people and why they are considered sacred.

One of my teachers referred to the elements as the Four Daughters of Beauty, and said that everything on earth is born out of the dance of these four daughters. We need always to take time to be awake to this beauty, and appreciate it.

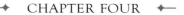

CHAPTER FOUR

THE ANIMALS

EARTH ANIMALS

The element earth gives form to all physical being—mountains, trees, plants, animals, and humans. Earth is feminine in its essence, although it is found in both women and men. It is characterized by gravity and substance. Its qualities are nurturing, strengthening, healing, balancing, providing, and teaching. The physical manifestation that earth offers us in the form of a body gives us the opportunity to learn and to grow. It is our choice if we use the gifts of the earth—food, shelter, tools, and clothing—to do good or to destroy. Our choices provide us with our learning and growing experiences. In her generosity and unconditional love, Mother Earth provides us with everything that we need to do what we choose. This is why native people see her as our sacred mother, who denies her children no experience.

The dense and heavy qualities of the element earth make it slower than air, fire, or water, and this can be observed in the character of the animals that are close to it. The bear, for instance, has true gravity. A bear usually moves slowly, and its small eyes reveal an awareness that is focused inward.

ANT

A S I WALKED up to an anthill in a forest in Germany, I immediately saw what I was looking for: a pile of little white stones. Ants frequently collect them, but biologists don't understand why—apparently they have no practical purpose.

I gave an offering to the ants and picked up fourteen of the white spirit stones for the rattle I was making.

Ants live in huge communities, which each one serves for the good of the whole. For ants, the group comes before the individual. Each ant has a specific function, and undertakes his task showing a high level of commitment, even a sense of duty.

Ant teaches that by patiently working together, and helping each other, we can accomplish great things. Through combined effort, ant builds extended, intricate dwellings above or below ground, a feat that would not be possible for an individual of its species.

The whole ant community thinks as one, and this phenomenon can also be observed among humans. Various communities of people have specific ways of defining reality and themselves, and members of the community are often in mutual agreement about them. This is the group mind and the group soul. What are important are the principles the conclusions are based on. In the shamanic tradition, the teachings of ancestors and of natural law guide the group mind, so there is an emphasis on living in harmony with the rest of creation. This is the message ant brings: when we follow the way of balance, our communities can be strong and healthy.

According to some esoteric schools of thought, ants have a healing and blessing effect on the Earth, restoring balance. Their antennae connect them to the air, the sky, and the rich world of smells to which they are highly receptive.

SPIDER

✻ WEB OF LIFE ✻ ONENESS ✻ KARMA

ONE MORNING IN DETROIT, I noticed a spider's web attached to my truck between the side mirror and the door. I left it there and set off on the long drive north on the interstate highway to visit my teacher. On my return home later on that day, I parked the truck and was about to walk over to my house, when I noticed that the web was still there and, what's more, the spider was still there, too. That's when I realized just how strong her web is.

Spider, the Great Weaver, weaves the web of life, the force that holds everything together, seen and unseen. People who are able to perceive this invisible web of life have found that it is similar to the spider's in construction.

Spider teaches us that all of life is connected, and that every action we take has an effect on the rest of life, just as touching one strand of her web will leave the

whole edifice quivering. A spider's web is like the Wheel of Life, or the Medicine Wheel. Her eight legs point in eight directions on the circle where all the powers of the universe are held.

Spider demonstrates the power of balance in the circular movement of all life. She is a reminder to us that when wise teachers such as the Buddha tell us that everything is one, they speak the truth.

Spider's medicine helps you to spin the web of your own life, your own reality. Her teaching emphasizes that we must do our groundwork carefully, in order to be able to build a strong foundation. Learn all the skills you will need in life, and once they are honed, always do your best. Then you can surrender to trust in the overall goodness and provision of life.

Spider teaches deep trust and surrender as she waits patiently in her web.

MOUSE

* TOUCH * TRUST * SENSITIVITY

IN A WOOD IN GERMANY, I was watching a mouse eating hazelnuts, surprised by her ability to penetrate their hard shells. Her rapid movements showed her nervousness but also her curiosity. It seemed as if her entire being was engaged in the experience of cracking open and eating those nuts.

Mouse is tiny and spends most of her time on the ground, using her heightened senses of touch, hearing, sight, and smell to explore and to search for food. Unlike hawk or eagle, who can see all their terrain from the sky, mouse experiences her environment directly and closely. This is her life. Only the immediate concerns her, and her sensitivity to her surroundings is acute, often manifested as emotional agitation, and sometimes even a visible pulse and heartbeat. Here lies mouse's lesson.

If we experience reality just through our mind, we can easily become aloof and distance ourselves from others. Alienation soon follows, which is the cause of much imbalance, illness, abuse, and destruction in the world. Call on mouse when you need to learn to touch life. Mouse teaches us to move from the rational mind into our sensory and emotional intelligences.

It is important for us to experience the whole range of human emotions: they make life richer and more fulfilling. Many people are afraid to allow their feelings to come to the surface because they've been hurt in the past. However, distorted emotions can be very destructive. Part of mouse's teaching is that, to avoid this, feelings must be given direction and trust must be our foundation. With her big, innocent eyes, mouse approaches the world with complete trust. In one shamanic teaching story, her trust eventually leads her to the Sacred Mountains, a destination we all ultimately seek to reach.

LIZARD

✳ DREAMING ✳ ILLUMINATION ✳ PROTECTION

I WAS RESTING on a bench in a Mexican churchyard, watching people amble past while others dozed in the shade, when I noticed a lizard running up the trunk of a tree in front of me. It stopped at my eye level, raising and lowering its body using its front and back legs simultaneously. Its colors merged with those of the tree bark until they were almost indistinguishable. The lizard's rhythmical movements and its otherworldly air began to lull me into a state of dreaming, so that I perceived the energies around me as much as the material forms of the physical world.

Lizard is the keeper of dreams. Blending into the background, she can become invisible and slip

from one dimension into another, like the shaman. She knows the trails that lead to dreams, visions, and images, and she can open the doorway to them.

On another afternoon in Mexico, a large iguana crawled toward me and proceeded to sit watching me for over an hour. I began to see the land and its people as they were hundreds of years ago. The iguana led me into dreaming, and gave me the gift of some beautiful images and teachings about the ways of the ancient peoples of Mexico. If you seek dreams and visions, ask lizard.

She basks in the sun to heat her body and blood, sourcing energy directly. The sun illuminates the world and warms the air. Lizard teaches us to seek the light that illuminates our minds and hearts, the light of spirit and truth. By absorbing and integrating that light and warmth, we awaken and become fully alive. Lizard shares these secret teachings.

Her body seems to rest in a permanent press-up, close to the earth, as if it pulls her. Her skin is dense and hardened, which gives her good protection. She has extreme endurance of thirst, and when in danger, she jettisons her tail. Its wriggling distracts her enemies, allowing her to escape.

MOLE

ELIZABETH, A WOMAN in her eighties, lived in the coastal mountains of northern California. In her garden she had 500 different varieties of daffodils and many fruit trees. Sometimes I would help her to look after them and one day, while I was doing some weeding and enjoying the exhilarating fragrance from some tiny daffodils, I caught a rare glimpse of a mole above ground.

I went over and picked her up and was surprised to find that her fur was so velvety. Even more surprising was the intense power in her small legs, which were designed purely for digging.

Mole builds long tunnels in the earth, where she spends her whole life in darkness. She may be blind, but mole senses and feels through direct contact with the soil. Her sight is that of the inner eye. Mole is the keeper of intuition. She brings us the message to look within and find our deep inner wisdom. Mole shows us the way through the tunnels of our mind to the place of knowledge, the safe and warm den, lined with grasses.

The mind can analyze and memorize but it is also the maze that can lead us into confusion. We don't always need to seek answers in the outer world. We can call on mole to help us journey to our heart, where there is clarity and peace. Her long nose points the way.

Regardless of her blindness, the mole's strong resolve and motivation enable her to build large complexes of tunnels. She is independent, and continues her work underground in the lower world, as she has done for thousands of years, without being influenced by what is going on above in the middle world, where she leaves traces in the form of mounds. If you see mole, remember to acknowledge your inner knowing.

SNAKE

* CREATION * LIFE FORCE ENERGY * RENEWAL

LATE ONE NIGHT I walked from my teacher's house over to the medicine house, where we held many of our ceremonies. As I opened the door and went to step inside, the sole of my foot touched something on the threshold—something living. Fortunately, I hadn't put my whole weight down, and so I raised my foot and carefully stepped to one side. Reaching a hand in and turning on the light, I was just in time to see a long snake with distinctive markings on its back slide away. It dawned on me that I had just stepped on a rattlesnake.

Snakes exude an air of intensity and mystery. Their eyes have a narrow range of expression and they seem unaffected by their surroundings, existing in a world apart from the one inhabited by humans.

In her constant bodily contact with the ground or with trees, snake stays close to the powers of creation, the life forces of Mother Earth. In Mexican spiritual tradition, Quetzalcoatl, the feathered serpent, represents the union of snake and quetzal, or eagle. Our ultimate task is to unite body and spirit, earth and sky, snake and bird. Learning and growing in our physical form should ultimately lead to illumination and union, the merging of opposites. Snake brings us these esoteric teachings, guiding us home.

In the concept of kundalini, the snake represents creative sexual energy that is curled at the base of the spine. When all our energy centers are open, the snake, or kundalini, can rise to the crown of the head in a direct awakening.

In life, our only certainty is that change is inevitable. By periodically shedding her skin, snake teaches us not to resist change, but to welcome renewal, even if it is painful initially. Change leads to growth, which is what we are here for.

SQUIRREL

∗ FORESIGHT ∗ INNER FIRE ∗ SHAMAN

AS A TEENAGER I used to watch a red squirrel that frequented a fir tree, the branches of which brushed our kitchen window. I could almost be in the squirrel's territory without disturbing her. I was fascinated to see her bury hazelnuts in our lawn in the fall, and then in winter, when food was scarce, I would watch her scrape away the snow on the ground and dig into the earth to find her stash of nuts.

Squirrel stores for the future because she knows what is coming. She understands the cycles of the year, and knows that fall, a time of full bellies with plenty of fruits and nuts on the trees, will be followed by winter's paucity. This is great medicine for human beings.

If you have observed squirrel for any length of time, you will know that she is like a coiled spring, full of latent acrobatic energy. Surefooted, she leaps from tree to tree through the forest canopy. Even sitting still, the swishing of her tail reveals squirrel's inner fire. One of my teachers told me his people's term for squirrel was Tree Lightning.

I have seen squirrels—black, red, gray— run vertically up the trunks of tall trees, then down again headfirst. This movement

is an important part of squirrel's medicine. The tree represents the Tree of Life, the World Tree. Its roots are the lower world, the realm of spirit animals and strong healing earth energies. Its trunk is the middle world, inhabited by humans, and its crown is the realm of gods and spirit teachers. Squirrel, traveling between spirit and human realms, represents the shaman, who does exactly the same. The purpose of this vertical journey is to bring messages and power from the spirit, so that we can learn to live in harmony and balance.

WEASEL

I T WAS A QUIET afternoon in Fall in a forest in Denmark. Leaves that had fallen from the tall oaks and beeches covered the ground with a dry carpet of yellows, browns, and reds. I was walking quietly, as I had been taught, placing my feet carefully on the ground, when I heard a sound off to my left. Something was moving fast across the dry leaves. I stopped instantly, next to the wide trunk of a beech tree, listening. At first I couldn't identify the source of the noise, but I noticed it was changing direction all the time, sometimes stopping for a moment, and then speeding up. Soon my patience was rewarded and I saw a weasel shoot across those dry leaves like a brown and white arrow, hunting, seeking her prey. Her small eyes were as black as night. I stood totally still by the old beech tree, watching her move closer and closer. The wind was in my favor and she didn't pick up my scent. All of a sudden she ran right past my foot, touching my shoe, and then disappeared into a small hole at the base of the tree. Everything became quiet again, as if she had never been there.

Weasel has speed, agility, and alertness, and is highly vigilant. Once, I was sitting on a stony mountain side where there seemed to be no sign of life, when suddenly a weasel appeared from a crevice between two rocks. She had been there all the time, aware of everything, and revealed herself only when she knew it was safe.

Her medicine is the ability to know all that is hidden. When you tell a story but leave out important details, weasel is not fooled. She sees what is hidden in the dark corners of your soul, all the things you don't want others to see, and those you might not even be aware of yourself. But she also sees your strengths and beauty. Weasel medicine can be a great asset for healers. Her assessments are accurate and to the point. In the Native American tradition, her powers were used to seek out the secrets of enemies.

Weasel is small, but she has a strong heart, and courage is one of her qualities. She will hunt animals much larger than herself. People who have watched a weasel run down and kill a big rat, or even a rabbit, will know what I mean. She is a warrior and should not be underestimated.

With her russet-colored back and white chest and belly, weasel blends in, and is difficult prey. Her ability to be invisible is part of her magic. Sometimes she likes to stay hidden and nurture her rich inner life.

POSSUM

ONE NIGHT WHEN DREAMING with the intention of meeting possum, I found myself watching a small group of them emerge from a tree hollow in the mystifying light of dusk. One by one, from high in the tree, they took off, gliding through the twilight over to the trunk of another tree. The sight filled me with wonder, and with a longing to be able to glide freely as they did.

High up in the foliage of the tree canopy is possum's world, just like squirrel in the northern hemisphere. There are many species of possum and some of them are so highly adapted to the tree-

tops that they have developed skin between their front and hind legs. When outstretched, this membrane enables them to glide from tree to tree, in some cases over distances of more than 300 ft (100 yds). Possums who don't have this aid take agile leaps from one tree to another.

Possum teaches the importance of being able to take flight and set your spirit free. She emphasizes the role of the shaman in a way similar to squirrel. Her tree canopy represents the Upper World, the sphere of higher consciousness where we are not restricted by physical reality. In bridging the gap from earth to air, matter to spirit, possum teaches the art of being able to function equally well in both the material world and the spiritual realm.

Her food consists of the sap and fruits of trees, and so she represents the knowledge of the Tree of Life.

She glides through the night like our soul in the dreamtime, like our spirit journeying out of body, seeing, hearing, and sensing with highly developed powers. Aboriginal tribes valued possum's skin highly both for its extremely soft fur and for its spiritual qualities.

RABBIT

* HUMILITY * ABUNDANCE * LOVE

WHILE WALKING EARLY one morning in the southwest of England, I saw several rabbits grazing. As I climbed a stile and dropped down into the next field, a hawk struck and killed one of the rabbits. The hawk began tearing at the flesh and very soon another hawk joined the feast. From where I stood, I could observe unnoticed the cycles of life and death, lifegiving, life-taking.

Rabbit is a great animal benefactor, and all predators, including humans, hunt rabbits in order to eat and live. The medicine of rabbit is humility—knowing your ability and your role, and accepting both happily. Rabbit knows exactly who she is and does not try to be more or less than that. The humility to be gained from learning simply how to be yourself is a wonderful quality. It brings freedom, grounding, and peace of mind, which are all

empowering qualities, even if you still need to be on the look out for danger.

There are many dangers for rabbit. The shadows that move swiftly across the ground may be hawks looking for a meal. Out in the bushes, foxes, weasels, and wolves may be stalking her. With her small body, rabbit can't fight back against her predators, but she still has defenses. Her strong legs give her the speed she needs to run for her den. Here, in the comfort of her home, she is safe, and here she keeps her young. Rabbit reproduces at a very high rate and can have several litters over the course of a summer. Like wild boar, this wealth of procreation gives her a role similar to that of Mother Earth, who provides abundantly for her children. Thus rabbit mates frequently, and love is another of her medicines.

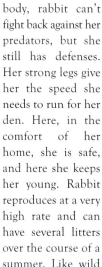

HARE

✱ INTUITION ✱ SOLITUDE ✱ SPEED

ONE NIGHT, BY THE LIGHT of a full moon, I was approaching a forest in Sjaeland, Denmark, when I noticed two hares out on the pasture. I stood still and watched them for a while. The night, the moonlit grass, and the long-eared, silent creatures generated an otherworldly feeling, almost as if I had begun to dream.

Hare is linked to the moon, which my teacher called the Chief of All Women. Both hare and the moon are feminine in their essence, and intuition is one of hare's main qualities. It is said that hares are the only non-predatory animals to take the risk of going out into the fields at night during full moon, when they can easily be spotted by those who might want to hunt them. If you watch the full moon for long enough, as you would on a vision quest, you might suddenly see hare jump across its surface.

She is associated with the moon goddess, who appears in many ancient spiritual traditions. The cycles of the moon are related to the cycles of women, as well as to those of death and rebirth.

Hare's elongated ears catch sounds that elude many other animals, yet her awareness is directed inward. She has self-containment and independence. She enjoys her own company and is solitary most of the time.

Her long, powerful hind legs carry her with lightning speed, saving her from hunters and predators. Running and speed are strong defenses, which are to be respected.

Those who have seen two hares standing on their hind legs to box will know that hares can also put up a good fight. They are fierce when it comes to defending their territory and setting boundaries.

CAT

AS I SAT ON A WOODLAND hillside in Cornwall, well hidden among some elder trees and brambles, watching and waiting, undetected, out of the corner of my eye I just caught something move down by the stream. Making sure I kept my head still, I swiveled my eyes and saw a black cat stalking. She froze, staring over in my direction as if she had sensed my presence. I remained completely still, and then she moved again, silently placing each paw on the soft earth by the stream, her body tensed with concentration. She was a domestic cat, but here in the woods she had become wild and free. It was as if I was watching a black panther; the distance between us, the perspective from above, and the shimmering light through the trees made the illusion appear more real.

Domesticated for thousands of years, cat somehow manages to remain free in spirit. She retains her inner life and walks her own untamed path. Cats can adapt to their original predatory life very quickly. Truly feral cats will not be tamed. Cat's message is to be independent no matter what your circumstances.

They are ruthless hunters. I have seen a small domestic cat return from a pond three hundred yards beyond the cabin where her owner lived, with a mallard duck lolling from her jaws.

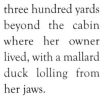

Cat's pupils contract and dilate like the shape of the moon, bonding her with it, and allowing her the gift of night sight. Everyone who has observed cat will have experienced the stare of a psychic, one who sees into realms beyond the physical and is suddenly roused by invisible presences. Cat medicine can help us to see in this way, and to move with stealth between physical and spirit worlds. Ancient peoples from Egyptians to Celts have recognized this art and all have held it sacred.

SKUNK

EGGS HAD BEGUN to disappear from the chicken coup at the medicine camp where I was living in the foothills of the Sierra Nevada. I began to watch the area, to see who was collecting them with such efficiency. One day a skunk walked past, quite close to where I sat. She obviously didn't feel threatened by me, relying on her reputation for being able to fight off any enemy with her foul-smelling liquid spray. She was right: I knew her reputation and left her alone.

Skunk gives three warnings before she sprays, temporarily blinding her opponent. The first is to stomp her front feet, the second is to turn around showing her tail, and the third is to lift her tail and aim. The teaching here is to heed warnings, preferably the first, and in this way avoid unnecessary conflict!

Warnings usually work only if you know there is power behind them, the ability to act if the warning is ignored. Skunk has proved she will back up her warnings with a highly effective assault on the senses. Anyone who has driven past a skunk that has been killed by a vehicle knows how over-powering the smell is. Skunk's reputation is her protection and her weapon because it demands respect. No one in their right mind would deliberately confront skunk. Consequently, she can enjoy life knowing she has the strength to handle the dangers and conflicts it might bring.

On the level of our consciousness, skunk teaches us to listen to the inner voice, or gut feeling, that always comes before we make a mistake, or take a decision we later come to regret. Often this voice is just a whisper, not easily heard against the loud voice of the mind.

RACCOON

I ONCE LIVED for several months on a farm in northeastern California. We kept geese, which were scrupulously locked up every night, but despite this two of them disappeared within a few days. The door to their pen had been opened, and I was commissioned to discover the thief. So the following night, I slept outdoors, close to the goose pen.

In the middle of the night, I was awoken by a resounding scream, and I rushed over to the goose pen, flashlight in hand, just in time to see a raccoon dragging a dead goose up a tree. As the raccoon moved from tree to tree, I followed on the ground. Suddenly, the goose dropped through the dark toward me, so close that I had to jump out of the way. When I looked up again, the raccoon was gone.

Raccoon is fast, clever, capable, and crafty. His black mask and his muted coloring allow him to move unseen at night, so that he can provide for himself and his family in situations where others would be at a loss. Raccoon is a trickster who brings us insight into what we need to understand. Shortly after the incident with the goose, I saw his young among the tree branches, and realized he needed the geese

to feed them, and I needed to put a lock on the goose pen.

Raccoon's paws look similar to human hands, and he uses them for highly specialized tasks, including opening animal pens and washing his food before eating it.

Just as raccoon is an expert at unlocking sources of food in the physical world, so he can unlock the spirit world for us. Call on raccoon if you need guidance to find the power you have lost, or given away, in the past. Even when you have lost part of your soul, raccoon's magic can help you bring it back.

MONKEY

✱ MOVEMENT ✱ INQUISITIVENESS ✱ SOCIAL EQUILIBRIUM

I WAS LOOKING OUT over a forested valley below the snow-capped peaks of the Himalayas, when a troupe of monkeys came leaping toward some nearby vegetable patches. These plots were tended daily by women from the village, and they must have been aware of their visitors because within minutes they ran out to chase them off.

Monkeys are full of energy, curiosity, and mischief. They are the acrobats of the forest, capable of moving with remarkable agility from tree to tree, using arms, legs, and tail. They teach us to wake up and explore life, to use all our resources, and to take every opportunity.

It is easy to sleep through life's adventure, and monkey tells us to awaken the child in us who gets up to mischief. This quality helps children to understand the world. Taking risks opens the door to the unknown, a door we must step through in order to learn and avoid stagnation.

Mischief indicates an appetite for life, an inner longing for exploration, fun, and adventure—although it obviously needs to be balanced and directed so that it doesn't harm others.

Being noisily vocal, monkey can be easily distracted by his own communicativeness, a lot like humans. There is a strong aspect of the trickster in monkey. He calls attention to the nature of our mind, and the need for us to discipline it through meditation and other practices that encourage a state of calm and inner stillness.

Living in groups, monkeys form tight-knit communities and practice the art of solving problems among themselves. Monkey can be consulted for help when equilibrium needs to be restored.

From the tree canopy, he sees events as they unfold in the forest, and when enemies stalk, he will sound an alarm call to alert all creatures.

FOX

WALKING THROUGH the woods on a hot summer's day in Denmark, I noticed a red fox curled up, sleeping in a warm spot between two beech trees. I moved toward her, using the method of stalking that I had been taught, and touched her gently with my foot. She opened her eyes and looked at me in a split second of disbelief, and then spun around and disappeared in the blink of an eye. Swiftness, surefootedness, and a quick mind that always knows what to do are all part of fox's medicine.

Foxes live in family units in which both parents feed and raise their young. Fox is balanced in this way, and exhibits both caring maternal characteristics and those of a warrior, a master of hunting and survival. She teaches us that gender equality helps to create a strong family. Fox embodies resourcefulness and daring in her quest to feed herself and her young.

Around the farmer's hen house, "the universe will always provide," is fox's philosophy.

Fox survives and flourishes because she is clever and adaptable; she is now found living in cities. Fox teaches us to be flexible rather than to resist change with a rigid attitude. Fox has a varied diet of plants, berries, meat, and whatever else comes her way. What we can learn from fox is not to let ourselves be held back by traditions and prejudices.

Foxes have an extraordinary vocal capacity and range, from strangulated screams to low barks. At night she speaks with her people, sending out her stories. This repeated calling and answering provides a model for us in resolving certain disputes, by listening while each side repeatedly presents its story, continuing until it is fully expressed and has been understood. This is the medicine way of the healing council.

BADGER

I WAS WALKING through a forest in Denmark, near my brother's house, at 4 a.m. The sun had just risen and the air was fresh and clear. Hearing a persistent rustling noise, I moved quietly toward the source to discover a badger, foraging among the debris on the ground. I stole forward to see how close I could get, but she became aware of my presence and turned to face me. Instead of fleeing, as I had expected her to do, she growled and charged. So there I was, running through the forest with a badger at my heels!

Badger has ferocity, endurance, and tenacity, and uses them partly to keep her boundaries clear. If you feel your space is being invaded by others, and it's difficult for you to say no, badger can help you. Healthy boundaries are necessary for self-respect. Aggression can be appropriate in certain situations. It can even save your life. Many people are uncomfortable with this power, but it is important to be able to awaken it when needed.

A little like bear, badger will spend the winter inside her warm burrow, dreaming and resting. She is close to the earth, spending much of her life underground, and she knows its secrets well. She digs deeply for roots, often sensing where they are in the dark, and her knowledge of plants makes her medicine useful in healing. Badger's strength and insight, and her quiet winter habits, teach the value of self-protection, slowing down, and looking after yourself, so that you can live in balance.

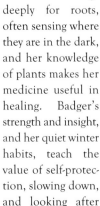

Badger is an architect; a badger's sett is a complex structure of underground tunnels leading to the den. Like fox, badger teaches us about the advantage of having more than one way into and out of situations. We need not be dependent on a single route but can take different paths to reach our destination.

DINGO

O N A DRUM JOURNEY, I saw a pack of dingoes gathered at night. In the darkness, the dingoes began howling and the howl became a song that covered the entire land. Those ancient voices seemed to express a deep belonging and inner wisdom, part of our heritage as human beings.

Dingo is a guardian, vigilant and alert to danger. Aboriginal tribes kept dingoes as watchdogs and companions, and they helped the people in many ways, including hunting with them and keeping them warm during cold nights. Dingo's ability to switch from being wild to domesticated speaks of intelligence and adaptability, and the amazing power those qualities bring. She can sense what is outside the circle of the camp, and has knowledge that humans have not yet acquired. Her ability to see into the otherworld means that she can warn of approaching negative energies. Her role as a guardian of the spirit world is similar to that of her cousin, the dog.

Dingoes are part of the same family as wolves, and live in packs that are organized very similarly. They form small, orderly communities where the dominant male and female are usually the only ones who breed. The other members of the pack help to bring up the pups. This structure is based upon each member having a specific role and all members cooperating to make the group as strong and efficient as possible. Community and working together are part of dingo's medicine.

Dingoes also use intelligent teamwork to hunt together. By adapting their strategies afresh to suit the animal being targeted, they can bring down prey as big as buffalo. Dingo is clever and potent.

In her role as a top predator, dingo holds a key position in keeping nature in balance, controlling the populations of her prey, and guarding the equilibrium of the land.

DOG

✳ SERVICE ✳ LOVE ✳ GUARDIAN

THE GOLDEN RETRIEVER I had as a teenager was strong, loyal, loving, and alert. He had an adventurous spirit, and was sometimes off exploring on his own for an entire day.

The alliance between dogs and humans goes back millennia. Genetically still close to wolf, dog gives up his freedom in order to help humans. Dog teaches us that living for other people, not just for yourself, helps the soul to evolve.

Dogs have guarded the camps of humans, carried their burdens, helped them hunt, found those who were lost, protected children, warned of danger, and

guided the blind. They provide comfort in times of loneliness and distress. Teaching by example, dog shows us that we can open the heart and practice love and compassion for the sake of good, not expecting anything in return. Dogs embody very high soul qualities, including loyalty. Abusive relationships must not be tolerated, whether between humans or between an animal and its owner, but dogs will forgive even abuse. This pure state of devotion is a precious gift, and we should never take advantage of it. Humans have bred some dogs inappropriately, to the point of cruelty both to other people and to the dog.

There is a particularly close bond between children and dogs. Both are pure in spirit and are not dominated by the rational mind.

Like wolves, dogs are pack animals. When they live with humans, we become their pack and their alpha females/males, whom they guard and defend. This role is not limited to physical existence. In the spirit world, dog guards the realm of the dead and helps souls to cross from the world of the living. In many spiritual traditions, a black dog guards the threshold between the two realms.

COYOTE

I WAS HIKING IN the Sierra Nevada foothills. Tall pines grew around me. The air bore the chill of early morning, but the sun was rising into a blue sky and promised a hot day. The trail curved around a wide trunk and there, up ahead of me on the track, watching me, stood a coyote, his bright, intelligent eyes delivering a look that pierced right through to my core. He seemed to be smiling.

Coyote is known as a trickster who forces us to adapt to unexpected situations. He repeatedly instigates change, one of the things we often resent. Evolving through change and trial is one of coyote's lessons. When our lives are comfortable, we tend not to learn much, but faced with adversity we develop, grow, expand, and move on to become the person we are supposed to be. Life is not meant to be trouble-free. Coyote represents a force in the cosmos that doesn't always act with integrity, but does result in the events we need in order for our souls to develop. That makes coyote a divine trickster. Sometimes he becomes caught in his own tricks, but he has an amazing ability always to find his feet.

Intelligence is another of his traits. Coyotes hunt together and trick their prey in countless ways. Howling outside a house, a coyote pack will deliberately alert, and thus locate, any dog in the vicinity. One coyote will approach the dog, enticing it to give chase, while all the time leading it farther away from cover and closer to where the rest of the pack waits to ambush its meal in safety.

Coyote is an excellent survivor who has repeatedly outwitted human efforts to exterminate him, and in this he offers great medicine: we cannot destroy him because he is a reflection of ourselves. Our enemies are often just our own projections. So next time you hear coyote sing, be ready for a new lesson, but trust that it is part of a greater plan.

KOALA

DREAMING ONE NIGHT, I came face to face with a koala. She was looking at me from the branch of a tree, slightly above my head. Her eyes were small and dark. As she stared in her slow, deliberate way, I felt she gave me the message to look within, and by doing so, I would know myself. Then she turned and climbed higher up into the tree canopy.

Eating only eucalyptus leaves from a select few species of trees, koala is capable of extracting nourishment from a very poor source, insufficient for other animals. She is known for her ability to live on virtually no water. In the now extinct Australian Aboriginal language, Dharug, the name for koala, means "doesn't drink." Koala has the medicine of being able to find sustenance where none seems to exist. This is a teaching on finding the value in small things.

Appreciation is an immensely powerful ability. If you can awaken it in yourself and be grateful for what you have, recognizing its true value, you begin to feel stronger. Appreciation transforms your outlook on life and is the route toward living in contentment and joy. Koala brings this wisdom.

Eucalyptus leaves contain high levels of toxic substances, but koala's extraordinary liver protects her against them. Koala shows you how to stop other people's toxic words from poisoning you. By knowing yourself, you can prevent their destructive effects on your body and mind.

The treetops are koala's realm. Here, close to the sky, she spends most of her time resting, sleeping, and dreaming by herself. She prefers to be alone and her awareness is completely inward most of the time. She climbs with slow, relaxed movements, entirely at her own pace. She teaches us to look within, and to dream. In this way, we can know ourselves.

BOAR

WHILE HIKING IN northern California early one morning, I came across a herd of wild boar, digging into the ground with vigor and enthusiasm. Their whole demeanor expressed will, determination, and single-mindedness.

Boar is a renowned game animal but he is different from most other big game. He possesses enormous strength, and his vast courage causes those who do consider hunting him to think twice.

When boar is confronted he will fight with incredible ferocity, and there is no enemy he will not face if challenged. He charges his opponent directly and won't back off. He will fight to the death, no matter what the odds are. Boar does not have the flexibility of the big cats or the speed of wolf, but his warrior qualities make up for the stiffness and lack of mobility that are part of his physical makeup. Boar teaches us to face up to our challenges, including our own weaknesses and fears. That is true courage.

Boar lives with honor, and will protect his family and kin with his life. It is the kind of honor that comes from being true to yourself, not the kind that comes from an inflated sense of self-importance. Boar teaches us never to give up, no matter how difficult the situation may appear to be.

In days gone by, when hunting was one of the main ways to find food, boar played an important role in providing meat for the people. Domesticated pigs continue to play this part. Wild boar, like pigs, have big litters of piglets and are therefore associated with fertility, and with its bounty and wealth. These qualities are similar to some of Mother Earth's attributes, and in this way boar, with his honorable ferocity and fertility, strongly encompasses both the masculine and the feminine.

MOUNTAIN LION

* BALANCE * COURAGE * INDEPENDENCE

I WAS WALKING DOWN a trail in the coastal mountains of northern California. It was early morning and it had rained during the night; the sandy ground between the pines and the manzanita bushes had been washed clean of all footprints. Then I saw fresh tracks. They were unmistakably those of a mountain lion. As I continued on my walk, I had a growing, and slightly disquieting, sensation of being watched. That night as I was lying in my tent, I heard a sound outside, like soft lapping of water. I stuck my head through the side door and saw the mountain lion drinking from a small pond about 30 feet away.

Mountain lion is the keeper of balance. She hunts and kills the weakest of the deer and other game, and in this manner helps create strength among them. The way she moves is the embodiment of balance, whether she is climbing trees or stalking high on rugged cliffs. Every muscle is under her smooth command; each paw is placed precisely and deliberately exactly where she wants it to be, without a sound. She divides her time between hunting and resting, spending long periods lying down doing nothing, and then stretching before she finally rises. And yet she is active as a hunter both night and day. Call on her to learn the art of balance, living equally from your heart, your feelings, your body, your mind, and your spirit.

Agility and suppleness are expressed in every step taken by a mountain lion. Her face conveys the hunter's strong inner forces of aggression and passion. She will hunt animals much larger than herself and defend her young with courage and fierceness.

Mountain lions live alone most of the time except during the mating season. The female raises her young by herself, not in prides together with other families. Mountain lion teaches you to be independent—to be your own leader, to trust yourself and your skills. A cub is taught stalking from a very young age, and after much trial and error, reaches adulthood having honed this skill to perfection. Mountain lion teaches the art of moving silently and invisibly.

JAGUAR

* SHAMAN * INTEGRITY * SELF-AWARENESS

ONE WARM SPRING afternoon I was sitting in the plaza in front of a pyramid in central Mexico, when a man I'd never met walked up and introduced himself by saying that his power animal was a jaguar. He said he wanted to show me something. He turned out to be from a lineage of shamans who had lived in the area for hundreds of years. During the next couple of hours, as we walked among the pyramids, I could see that everything about him mirrored the big cat. That day he gave me insights into the mysteries of how people had worked with the pyramids in ancient times.

The jaguar and the shaman are closely related in the Mexican and South American spiritual traditions. They were often considered the same, and many shamans had the ability to shape shift into a jaguar and travel in its form, in physical reality as well as in other dimensions. Jaguar's medicine can take you into the realm of strong, mystical powers within and beyond yourself. By understanding the nature of these powers you can alter reality. Healing can take place, and events can be encouraged to happen, while others can be discouraged from occurring. You can connect with the incredible energies of Mother Earth, and travel in time and space.

Jaguar sees in the dark of night and in the dark of veiled worlds. He stalks on the earth, climbs up trees toward the sky, and, unusually, is drawn to play in water. His roar announces his presence like a blaze of fire. He works on all elemental levels.

The immense powers of jaguar mean that he carries the heavy responsibility of always using them with the highest integrity. Jaguar teaches us to keep our hearts pure and to use our power wisely. Power can be used to heal or destroy. The choice is yours. With power comes temptation. We can be seduced by our own knowledge and ability. Jaguar guides you to use integrity as your measure. He asks: "Do you have people's highest good in mind when you act, or are you being seduced by your ego?"

Jaguar prowls silently, undetected, knowing when to move and when to wait, closing in on his prey, waiting for the right moment to strike. Call on jaguar to learn to stalk yourself. Understanding yourself begins with self-observation. Just as jaguar stalks his prey, you can begin to observe yourself throughout the day. What are your habits? What triggers your emotional

reactions? When do you doubt your abilities? How often do you judge yourself? And others? Observe yourself without judgment, as jaguar does not judge the deer he stalks. Observation should be as impartial and clear as possible.

When you have stalked yourself for a while, you can begin to transform the habits, thoughts, and judgments that are not leading you toward the best you can be. Then you begin to change, guided by the wisdom of jaguar.

WOLF

I WAS SNOWSHOEING through a forest in northern Michigan one evening and the moon was close to full. Nearing a frozen river, I stopped, took off the snowshoes, and leaned up against a pine tree. Snow deepened the silence, which was suddenly broken by a long, astonishing cry that filled the air with enchanted reverberation: the howl of the wolf.

Wolf travels the land with her keen senses primed. She covers long distances with great speed, lightly and silently. She knows all trails. Call on her if you are lost, or if you want to explore new territories, or find another direction in your life. She is a pathfinder, bringing back accurate information, so that you can make informed choices. In Native American sign language, the signs for wolf and scout are the same.

Wolf will show you the shortest distance between waterholes, so that you don't waste time and energy. She teaches how to survive intelligently, how to be focused and clear.

Wolf packs are highly organized so that individuals successfully cohabit, showing mutual respect. Wolf teaches us how to live together. The organization of some Native American tribes was inspired by wolf societies. Wolf shows us how important it is to have a strong family where there is support and devotion. Yet he also teaches that at times it may be appropriate to choose the freedom of solitude, becoming a lone wolf to sort things out. Reflecting alone may lead to clarity.

Wolf sings to the moon, the Chief of All Women, and has the power of intuitive wisdom. This counsel is to be sought when the mind does not have a clear answer. When you find it, let your voice sound pure and strong, like wolf singing toward the sky, up to Grandmother Moon.

KANGAROO

I WANTED TO MEET and learn about kangaroos, and decided to try to do so on a drum journey. I saw a herd bounding across sparsely wooded, arid earth, with an effortless regularity to their pace. The way they moved revealed a complete adaptation to the elements, and unity with the land they inhabited. At one point, they reached a lake and began swimming across it, unfazed by the water. I was fascinated and wanted to learn more.

Leaping is one of kangaroo's medicines. With the aid of her powerful hind legs, she can travel long distances at high speed, using

very little energy. She is able to conserve her resources very effectively. Her endurance is also shown by her ability to survive for a long time without water, and on a meager diet of grasses and herbs.

Among other unique qualities, kangaroo is able to halt the development of an embryo in the womb until the young joey

she is already carrying in her pouch is able to leave its safety for short periods. Kangaroo can have an embryo in the womb, its development frozen, a tiny joey in the pouch, suckling on a teat that is producing the right kind of milk for a newborn, and an older youngster peering out of the pouch, almost ready to leave permanently. She will still be feeding the older baby but from another teat that produces milk more suitable for the youngster's needs.

This sense of timing is reflected in kangaroo's ability to adjust mating and reproduction according to the seasons and weather, to make sure she can support newborns. Reproduction and fertility are powerful aspects of kangaroo's medicine.

Kangaroo is nocturnal, linked to the moon and the feminine. It is usually the female who warns the group of danger by stomping her feet, sending the herd toward safety.

DEER

SKIING THROUGH the woods in Jutland, in Denmark, I came to the edge of a field where some deer, about six of them, were scraping away the snow to find grass. The wind had picked up, it was snowing, and the deer had not heard me coming. They were as surprised as I was.

I was familiar with the deer of this area. They were wild, always alert, and it was very unusual to get so close to them. They all raised their heads and looked at me, but they didn't run as I had expected them to do. They stood and watched. Then a doe began to walk toward me, every muscle in her body tensed, one short, quick step at a time. She stood right in front of me for a moment, then turned, and ran into the woods. Within seconds the whole herd was gone, as if it had never been there. Only the tracks testified that they had not been apparitions.

Deer has the magic of being able to disappear. You can see a deer standing between the trees, and in the blink of an eye she is gone without trace. Hunters know this well. Most of the time, deer's world is to be found in dimly lit woods, in the mysterious realm between the trunks of trees, which is full of fine fragrances, and where sounds are different from out on the open land.

Deer's big, dark eyes reveal the gentleness that is part of her medicine. Her slender legs hold her body high off the ground. Her long neck holds her head with an air of grace. The male's antlers reach toward the crown of the trees.

Deer gives her life so that others can live. Humans are among those who have received deer's gift throughout time, along with big cats, wolves, eagles, and many others. With her highly sensitive ears, which can swivel in multiple directions, deer teaches us alertness. She listens acutely, and sniffs every scent on the air, poised ready to run. She displays the vigilance of the hunted with grace, gentleness, and peace.

REINDEER (CARIBOU)

✳ EQUALITY ✳ BALANCE ✳ FRUGALITY

HIKING BEYOND the Arctic circle in Norwegian Lapland, where I visited a Sami friend who shared some of her teachings with me, I often came across reindeer. They roamed in small herds, stopping to feed every so often. They exuded self-contentment, as if resigning themselves to their existence and their fate.

The open tundra of the far north, forests, and high mountains are the home of reindeer. The wide expanse of land, where trees never grow very tall, has helped shape their long bodies and short legs. Their wide hooves allow them to walk safely over snowbound landscapes. Unusually among deer, both males and females have antlers, which they shed and regrow each year. Reindeer are keepers of balance and equality. While the females are pregnant, during the winter, their antlers are at their tallest. They shed them in spring or early summer, just around the time the calves are born. The males' antlers are at their strongest during the rut, in the fall, and they shed them during the winter.

Reindeer's Arctic home is bathed in the midnight sun during the summer, but in the middle of winter, either side of the solstice, darkness reigns. Then only the moon and stars shine light on the snow-covered land. This balance of opposites is apparent in reindeer's powerful antlers and gentle eyes.

Reindeer migrate in small herds toward coastal areas in the summer, returning inland before winter sets in. They then form vast herds to roam the land, and scrape away the snow in patches, in search of lichens and reindeer moss on which to feed. At this time, they develop an extra layer of fat under the skin and a soft undercoat of thick, insulating fur for protection from the bitter cold. Reindeer teaches us to use well the few resources we have at our disposal.

Reindeer has given a great gift to the Sami people of Russia and northern Scandinavia by allowing herself to be domesticated. For the Sami, her medicine is similar to that of buffalo. She is the provider of food, shelter, rich fatty milk, tools, and clothing. This sacrifice of her freedom is her biggest offering and is a lesson in compassion and selflessness.

ELK

I T WAS EARLY FALL and the sun was bright. I stood at the edge of a wood, watching a herd of elk in a field. The females grazed. The male stood with his head raised, absorbing through his nostrils any information that had been carried on the wind. He was guarding his flock. The huge antlers seemed like solidified rays of light reaching up toward the sun.

The elk and the European red deer are very similar creatures, and they carry similar medicine.

Elk owns his territory. He embodies masculine power and sexuality, and purveys strong, warrior medicine. He has fought to win his flock of females and will defend them. Elk teaches pride in yourself and your power. He can help you to accept and express male sexuality. Elk also teaches us to balance these qualities with humility, so that male power becomes natural and healthy, rather than nurtured merely to feed an inflated ego that needs attention. After the rutting season, elk sheds his antlers and joins a herd of male companions, with whom he spends the rest of the year.

Here elk shows us the vital importance of spending time with friends of your own gender, people who support each other rather than try to compete. Learning to be together in a genuine way with your friends can make a big difference to the quality of your life. Elk teaches you to believe that you can open up your heart and share.

Among native people this has played a major role in social organization. It means that the circle of men must be strong and whole, as must the circle of women. When men and women can come together as well-adjusted groups, the circle of people will be strong.

MOOSE

KAYAKING IN THE WILDERNESS early one morning, I saw a moose standing in the clean still waters of the lake, chewing on green reeds. He was massive and powerful. There was something primordial about him, and if it hadn't been for my fiberglass kayak, the scene could have been a thousand years old.

Moose is the keeper of the wisdom of stones. Ancient stones that have been here since the beginning know everything that has happened on Mother Earth. They hold the wisdom of the soul. Those that lie under the surface of the water represent the wisdom held deep inside the subconscious mind in the fertile mud that emerges where earth and water, substance and feeling, meet. By eating the reeds, the roots of which entwine them, moose absorbs the wisdom of the stones.

He is mysterious and at the same time pragmatic. He teaches us to be still and seek the guidance of ancient voices, and to find our own inner strength and express it without fearing to be seen and heard. All this comes from centeredness, and not from a position of needing attention.

Like elk, the male moose is a warrior who trusts himself and is proud to be male.

His legs are long and strong, rooted to the earth, and at the same time they raise him toward the sky. His big nose enables him to breathe in the sensory information around him, and from his crown center, heavy antlers reach out and connect him to the cosmos. His bellowing voice can be heard throughout the forest during the fall mating season, letting everybody know he is there, bringing the seed of life.

BEAR

I WAS HIKING through some woods in northern California, near the home of a Native American Indian who was my teacher at the time, when I suddenly stood face to face with a large black bear. We both stopped in our tracks and stared at each other. Now, I knew I shouldn't stare into a bear's eyes, but there was something about that black bear that compelled me to do it anyway. I felt completely safe. We stood there for what seemed a long time. Then the bear turned and bounded up a steep hill; she was at the brow of it in a moment. That was when I realized how strong a bear is. There was no way I could have outrun her.

My meeting with the black bear was a medicine encounter, and even now, twenty years later, I can feel, and tap into, the power of that animal. She is closely linked to the element earth, and her inner qualities are present in her physical form. Bear medicine is solid strength, grounding, and taking one step at a time. Bear is excellent for people who may feel unstable in life. She has gravity, weight, and is generally slow in her movements, although she can be very fast if she chooses; and she can stand and walk upright on her back legs, which brings her mysteriously close to humanity.

Another of bear's medicines is symbolized by her spending winter in the dream state. In the summer and fall she stores enough body fat to fast through the cold months, while she hibernates. She looks into the dark and knows the secrets of the night. Bear offers strong protection in the subconscious realm, as she enters the deep layers of the mind during that long introspective time while ice and snow cover the ground. Those who need help to sharpen their dreaming skills can call on bear.

Bear may appear lumbering and furry, but you don't want to be on the receiving end of her wrath if you have crossed her boundaries or threatened her young. She is the non-sentimental female who turns into a ferocious warrior when the need arises. She can be unpredictable, and it is wise always to respect her.

Above all else, bear medicine is that of healer. When she emerges in early spring, she seeks and digs up herbs that will cleanse and activate her digestive system. She knows the secrets of healing plants, and if you dream of bear, you are being called to walk the path of a healer in one form or another. Shamans and healers often have bear as a power animal or spirit helper.

HORSE

FROM A DISTANCE I could see the herd grazing. The vegetation was mainly sagebrush, and these tough, wild horses had learned to survive in the harsh desert of Nevada. As I tried to get closer, one horse took a few steps forward and faced me. He was the lead stallion, protecting the herd, and he seemed to be the essence of everything that is horse. Lifting his head proudly, he looked strong, courageous, wild, and free. Eyes watchful, ears raised, he faced the world, ready to act, seeming to embody the power of the sun.

A galloping horse, thundering across the land—his movement flowing and graceful, the wind blowing his long mane and tail—represents the spirit of freedom. Despite his heavy body, horse flaunts his qualities of speed and endurance as he moves swiftly over long distances. Horse teaches us to send our spirit galloping toward liberty, and not to be weighed down

by restricting beliefs and everyday routines. Your unconquerable spirit is the one thing that can set you free.

Horse gave humans an enormous gift when he became domesticated. Letting us ride upon his back, he allowed us to taste his independence, enabling us to travel far and fast. He carried our loads, pulled the plough, and transformed our lives and our world. Horse brought wealth and power. Humans owe him a great deal. His medicine is therefore also that of sharing and compassion. Putting the welfare of others first is one of his noble qualities. If we meditate on the sacred agreements between horse and humans, we may begin to understand this.

Through the ages, horse has carried shamans into the world of spirit, and this tells us of his mysterious power. He is psychic and can warn you of storms and other natural phenomena.

BUFFALO (BISON)

ABUNDANCE ✽ STRENGTH ✽ DETERMINATION

A S I WALKED ON the plains in South Dakota following the roll of each gentle hill, I saw a buffalo, or bison, lumbering in my direction through the dry grass yellowed by the summer sun. Immediately I stepped off the trail to signal that I was making space for the buffalo to pass.

I noticed that he was a burly, heavy bull, crowned with swathes of curling hair between his horns and a mane that grew dense and shaggy across his chest. When he had advanced a little farther along his path, he must have caught wind of me, because he stopped a few yards away, and glared directly at me. I realized this bull could mow me down with ease if inclined, or provoked, to do so, and averted my eyes, trying to avoid direct contact with his fierce glare. But the buffalo's keen sense of smell compensates for his poor eyesight, so it was unlikely he could see my eyes in much detail anyway. The two of us stood in each other's presence, the big bull breathing loudly in and out through black nostrils, for what felt like a very long time, and then he began to walk on.

In the past buffalo provided many people with what they needed for survival: food, shelter, tools, and clothing. This was especially so for the Plains Indians of North America. In huge, highly visible herds, which grazed at a leisurely pace across the grasslands, buffalo gave readily of herself so that others could live, and this endows her with the medicine of sacrifice.

Buffalo is like Mother Earth who gives her children everything they need. She gives generously and abundantly, and in return we must always remember to give thanks and to show our gratitude and respect. We should never take her gifts for granted. One day they may not be here, just as the buffalo virtually disappeared in Europe, and was exterminated across North America until breeding programs began to reintroduce the breed after 1900.

Another quality of the buffalo is strength. This was perfectly clear when I stood face to face with that bull on the prairie. The impression I had was that nothing could stop him, that with his power and endurance he could walk through anything. I also sensed his unpredictability. His massive bulk, frozen in concentration before me, had a latent power that could be unleashed at any moment. The bull embodies kinetic energy, strong and primordial as lightning. Ancient people

perceived this mysterious power, and expressed their respect through ceremony in buffalo societies.

Buffalo can move faster than a horse to reach speeds of around 35 miles (56 km) an hour. However, most of the time she is slow, heavy, and dense, like the earth. Her eyes are small and her awareness is very much inside herself. Buffalo has the demeanor of one who feels safe and at peace.

AIR ANIMALS

The element air is invisible, yet surrounds us at all times. We live in an ocean of air. Fast-moving, it can change direction easily, like the mind with its ever-changing thought patterns. Air is light and free, lacking the gravity of the earth. Masculine in its fundamental nature, although it is present in both women and men, it brings cleansing and clarity. Air carries messages in the form of sound and smell, and animals are continuously tuning in to it to receive the information they need for survival. Thus air and wind are connected to the power of wisdom and knowledge. The wind carries our prayers, and the smoke from incense and herbs is like prayer made visible.

Air is a mysterious power hiding within it the vitality and life force that we receive through breath. We die if we are cut off from it for very long. For us, it is truly the breath of life, and is connected to our spirit. In many languages, the words for spirit and breath are the same, or very similar. In some of the old tribal cultures, the hunter would crouch down to take in the last breath of the deer he had killed, so that part of its spirit would continue to live within him.

LADYBUG

ON THE SLOPING WALL of a house in rural Italy, a praying mantis waited for an approaching ladybug. As it drew near, the mantis struck, unfolding its powerful claws and swiping the ladybug to its mouth. But the mantis dropped its prey within seconds, wincing visibly, its head drooping as it slid backward down the inclined surface of the wall. The ladybug had released her defense, a bitter chemical, toxic enough to disable a praying mantis.

Ladybug is an effective protector of plants as well as of her own safety. She and her larvae will eat large numbers of aphids, to the delight of gardeners. Once a plant has been cleared of aphids, the ladybug moves to the next. One of the teachings she brings is to protect what nourishes us, whether food, nature, books, music, art, love, spiritual practice, or exercise.

The common ladybug has seven black spots on her red back. Seven is a sacred number, the significance of which varies according to spiritual tradition. I was taught that it represents the seven directions that define the world, the universe, and each individual: sky, earth, east, south, west, north, and center. Shamans see human existence as the Sacred Dream of Life; the seven directions hold us and give us orientation and guidance within this Dream. Ladybug teaches us to call upon our seven directional forces and to step onto the path of awakening to free ourselves from the spell of illusion.

During winter, ladybugs hibernate together in groups under stones and bark, and in other sheltered places. This time of sleep and stillness brings dreaming and introspection to ladybug's medicine.

Tradition has it that ladybug has been bestowed with the ability to carry prayers upward to the Creator, especially in relation to the weather.

BEE

ON ONE WARM MIDSUMMER'S day I was teaching at an outdoor workshop in Ireland. Suddenly, we heard a humming that grew louder and louder. There was something unreal about the sound, and everyone instinctively turned to face the direction it was coming from.

We stood there in awed silence as a dark cloud emerged from the woods and flew right over our heads—a crescendo of thousands of bees, humming a mystical song. The swarm was gone as quickly as it had come, leaving us amazed by the impact we had felt from its brief visit.

Bees live in matriarchal societies, and are dedicated to ensuring the survival of their queen. The swarm that flew over our circle was led by a queen bee on her mission to find a new home. Bee teaches us to honor the feminine, the goddess, from whom all life is born.

Bees collect pollen, to feed their larvae, and nectar, with which they make honey. Many flowering plants and trees rely upon bees for reproduction—while collecting pollen on their furry bodies, bees also distribute it from flower to flower.

Like ants, bees are of one mind and they live in harmonious, organized communities: each has a role to play and is committed to working for the benefit of the hive. The sting of bee is painful, and others know to respect these insects.

As bee moves from one flower to the next, she represents the diversity of life. Bee teaches us to drink the nectar of all experiences. Brought from all directions into the hive, the nectar is transformed into honey, a powerful healing and antibacterial substance.

When their work is done at the end of the year, the bees all die, except the queen, who survives winter. Through the Great Mother, life is reborn.

BUTTERFLY

✳ TRANSFORMATION ✳ JOY ✳ SOUL

THE OUTSIDE OF THE arbor provided shade from the intense midday heat. I was at a Lakota Sundance, and I had brought some questions to an elder whom I was meeting for the first time. We sat facing the hills and, as he spoke, a butterfly flitted past, in front of our faces. The elder stopped his flow of words and looked at me: "Your teachers have taught you to pay attention. Pay attention to the butterfly! She brings the message of transformation." Our conversation over the past few minutes had revolved around transformation, and the butterfly had confirmed the elder's words.

From egg to caterpillar to cocoon to butterfly, the life of this beautiful insect is one of transformation. She shows us that we too must transform ourselves. We must grow and eventually break out of the cocoon to become our true selves, in all our beauty as human beings.

Our soul is like the butterfly, delicate and light, taking flight on the winds of internal evolution, growing, expanding, learning, traveling, and returning home to the Great Mother, having drunk the nectar of life.

Butterfly is free, flying from one flower to another, curious about life, trusting, full of joy. With her long antennae, butterfly reaches out toward the cosmos and absorbs the fragrances of the air. She opens her colorful wings to the sun, with whom she is intimately linked. Butterfly soaks up light and heat, and takes off into the air to be closer to the sun, closer to the light.

Butterfly dances through life with ease. She is always ready to change direction, bringing the message that we must slow down and see the magic around us, and appreciate the beauty of life. Butterfly knows that life is short and that each moment counts.

DRAGONFLY

✱ MESMERIZE ✱ ALL POTENTIAL ✱ TRUE SELF

IN THE MAGICAL LAND of Mexico, where dreaming and reality often merge, I was on the beach one afternoon near the pyramids at Tulum. All of a sudden I became aware of a colorful dragonfly. Soon, many more joined it, flying back and forth in front of me. Hypnotized by their dance, I was filled with a sense of mystery.

Those iridescent wings can mesmerize us, altering our consciousness and taking us into a shimmering world. This is the realm of soul. Dragonfly's first teaching is to make space for mystery.

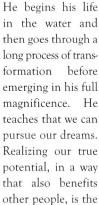

If we remain locked in our rational mind, we lose touch with our heart, soul, and spirit. Rationality and logic dominate modern western culture, but do not help us to identify our authentic purpose. Dragonfly encourages us to see the illusions that define us. Let him guide you to the forgotten part of your soul, so that an understanding of your true self can begin to emerge.

Dragonfly often hovers in one place, held there by the rapid movement of his wings. From this still center he moves up, down, backward, forward, left, right. These are the seven directions: the sky, earth, east, south, west, north, and finally center. This shows that dragonfly is the keeper of potential. He begins his life in the water and then goes through a long process of transformation before emerging in his full magnificence. He teaches that we can pursue our dreams. Realizing our true potential, in a way that also benefits other people, is the ultimate expression of the power of the dragonfly.

Dragonfly is extremely difficult to catch, and this ability, combined with his astonishing swiftness and accuracy when he hunts insects in the air, makes him a superior warrior. If you need help with battles you are fighting, or with goals you want to accomplish, call on dragonfly.

SWALLOW

SITTING HIGH ON A CLIFF in Wyoming, I was surrounded above, below, and on all sides by swallows—adults and young. Their bright spirits, high-pitched song, and sweeping flight against blue sky and red rock seemed to enhance the warmth and light of the sun. Some of them flew just above my head. I felt cleansed and blessed by their presence.

Swallow is a migratory bird, flying from the south to announce the arrival of spring. She brings a message of renewal, and with it inspiration and optimism. The hardships of winter are over and the renewed power of the sun promises life and plenty. As a bird of the sun, linked to its rhythm, swallow's song expresses the light within. When she flies from the southern to the northern hemisphere in spring, she seeks longer days and shorter nights. In the increased sunlight, her reproductive urge is kindled and she brings forth new life.

Swallow is a messenger of the spirits. Some North American Indian tribes have called her "starbird," and Ancient Egyptians saw swallows as being strongly linked to the ancestral realm. She signifies the power to resurrect light and life, as she heralds their return. Swallow can show the way, traveling thousands of miles to find the same nest year after year. She can guide us toward light, clarity, and illumination.

Swallow moves in her element of air with startling swiftness, efficiently hunting insects in curving flight. North American Indian people have also called her the "little bird goes to war." Dexterous and hard to target, she embodies a strong warrior power and is hard for other animals to hunt.

In low pressure, swallow knows to seek insects close to the ground, and in high pressure she rises accordingly. So her flight can predict the weather.

HUMMINGBIRD

✳ JOY ✳ BEAUTY ✳ LOVE

THE SUN HAD RISEN a few hours earlier, traveling across the sky as the earth continued its orbit. A humming sound came faintly from the east, and I turned to see what this muted buzzing could be. A bright shape shot westward like a dart and I caught a glimpse of something red and iridescent, but it disappeared in an instant, only to appear in the south for a brief moment, not long enough for me to see what it was. It moved again and this time appeared in the north, hovering in the air right in front of me. Then I had no doubt. I had seen my very first hummingbird on my first visit to the United States.

Hummingbird brings a smile to the face of most who see her, and fills people with a sense of joy. She dances among the flowers, hovering in mid-air to drink the nectar, her wings fluttering too fast for the eye to see. Her hum and her song are ethereal, and induce a slight trance. Her bright sparkling colors glimmer in the sunlight.

Hummingbird is so delicate, beautiful, and joyful that she can seem too bright and fair for the world we live in. She brings beauty and blessings from the world of spirit into our consciousness, and when we see her dance and drink from the flowers, we remember, deep within ourselves, the beauty of our true spiritual home. The joy hummingbird evokes in us flows from her reminder of who we truly are. The home of our spirit is much like the bright light of the sun, the flamboyant beauty of flowers, the sweet fragrance of nectar, and the trilling dance of hummingbird.

She opens our hearts and helps us to feel love. She shows us that we can move in all directions if we surrender to the way of beauty. This means to live in a way that is founded on respect and gratitude for all life.

Hummingbird has a very light body, because she stores no fat. She is vulnerable and fragile, and relies on the rays of the rising sun to give her sufficient energy to move from flower to flower. The way of beauty is also a delicate balance. One of the hardest things for us to do is to retain the level of subtle awareness that will enable us to seek balance and to readjust when it is lost so that we can re-establish it.

Joy and beauty are vulnerable and easily lost. Keeping them requires us to be in touch with vulnerable parts of ourselves and to accept them. It means being responsible for ourselves and taking risks, but as hummingbird shows, this can create beauty.

WOODPECKER

* WARRIOR * DRUMMING * WAVES

ONE WINTER'S AFTERNOON when I was skiing in the woods in western Denmark, I noticed a big anthill that had a fresh hole on one side. I was just a child and curious, so I slid over to look at it more closely, bending down to take a good look while keeping the skis on my feet. The moment I stared into the hole there was a shrill scream, and a huge woodpecker burst from inside the anthill. Needless to say, I was as terrified as the woodpecker.

Tapping trunks with his strong beak, woodpecker reaches in to where insects have bored holes and are hiding. He can penetrate both old dead wood and new fresh wood with the tremendous power of his beak and neck. His medicine is that of a warrior. Some woodpeckers have a red patch on top of their head, the color of honor. When that woodpecker fled the anthill, I felt his war cry directly!

You can call on woodpecker if you need to break through the surface of a situation and reveal what is at the core. This is one of his medicines.

Woodpecker is the drummer of the forest. His rhythmic beat summons spiritual powers in nature. The call of the drum reminds us that we can alter our consciousness and enter meditative and shamanic states of expanded awareness. The drumming can take us on a journey by helping us to perceive different layers of reality and the spiritual forces that lie behind physical forms, whether in woods or cities.

Woodpecker's undulating flight teaches us about our existence. We will encounter many ups and downs while we journey through life, and we must remember to see them for what they are. A dip is just a dip: you will rise again.

BAT

* REBIRTH * DREAMING * UNION

AS A CHILD I WOULD watch bats hunting insects on summer nights. They invoked a sense of mystery, and I wondered where they came from because I never saw them in the daytime, and never found their nesting place. Their flight was quite different from that of birds—rapid, with abrupt flicking turns and dips. If I threw stones up in the air in front of them, the bats would react instantly and change direction.

During the day, bats spend most of their time in caves and other dark places. They hang upside down when they sleep and rest, just like unborn babies in the womb, waiting for the moment of birth.

Emerging at night, bat brings us the message of rebirth. The cave is the womb of Mother Earth. Bat counsels you to enter the darkness of transformation—let the old die, spread your wings, and fly into the new. Be reborn, stronger and wiser.

Birth can be painful, but there is no life without it. Bat teaches that we must go through death and rebirth over and over again as part of our journey here on Earth. When bat hangs upside down waiting for birth, she is dreaming of what she can become. We too must dream before we can

fulfill our destinies, until the time comes to stop dreaming and take action.

Most bats live in large communities, leaving and returning to the cave at much the same time. Thus bat teaches us to be united. Constant separation and isolation are not good for human beings. They disrupt our balance, setting us apart from the rest of creation and making us lonely. Union gives us a sense of belonging, creating strength.

CROW

ONE DAY IN FALL I was standing under an alder tree by the lakeshore as dusk fell and crows began to gather. They came from all directions, flying in from the feeding areas where they had spent the day, and soon about 150 of them filled the trees around me. I found their sense of timing impressive. As they each found a perch in the trees, they were all talking loudly among themselves. Purely by accident, I found myself in the right place at the right time to experience a crow council.

Crows are the keepers of the council. The council is an ancient method of decision-making, allowing everyone's voice to be heard. All those at the council listen carefully to what everyone else has to say, and then a decision is made based on consensus. The council ensures that people are united and consequently strong, as opposed to divided, which is often the case in modern societies. Thus crow is a good medicine to call on when you need to make decisions with your partner, family, or community.

In order for the council to work, everybody has both to listen and to speak from the heart, really taking in what others have to say. The decisions coming out of the council should be for the good of all. Council principles are based on natural law and the law of the divine, of which crow is the guardian. In the same way as you would listen when raven speaks, listen carefully when you hear crow caw, because she often brings important messages.

Crow is also keeper of the art of shape shifting, whereby shamans have traditionally changed forms, for instance becoming an animal and then traveling as that form to discover, explore, or deliver a message.

FALCON

A BIRD WAS SITTING on top of the cliffs about 800 yards ahead. It was too far away to identify, but there was something about it that held my attention. This bird was different from any of the others I'd seen that day. It exuded authority. As I got closer, it took off, and once airborne, its long, pointed wings, rapid flight, and distinctive hooded head revealed its identity: a peregrine falcon.

No other bird or animal can match the speed of a peregrine. When hunting, he usually strikes his prey on the wing. Diving from above, he hits it with his breastbone at such velocity that he is known to have cut a duck in half in mid-air.

Falcon teaches that if you are going to strike, then strike with appropriate force. Put your full intention into what you do and do it properly. The birds hit by falcon die immediately and without suffering.

Sometimes being nice and gentle does not do anyone good service.

The lesson is to do things wholeheartedly, whatever you are attempting. If you are a leader, take charge and be the leader. If you serve others, step fully into that role and give it all you can. Be focused, do your best, and then life becomes more enjoyable.

The "tooth" on the side of falcon's beak is perfectly evolved for his eating habits and hunting style. It tells us about the importance of having the right kind of tools and skills for whatever task we may take on.

Falcon's black eyes can look through the veil of different realities and perceive other dimensions. He escorts the soul of the dead on their journey to the otherworld. From his vantage point high above the ground, nothing is hidden from his sharp eye.

RAVEN

I WAS HIKING through a steep gorge leading down to the sea on the southwest coast of Crete. Aged pines and cedars grew on both sides of the narrow trail, which was strewn with rocks. The air was dry. I heard a deep hoarse voice above me, and looking up, I saw a large, lustrously black raven circling overhead, without any movement of its wings. Then two ravens were drawing the ancient symbol of a circle on the blue sky, occasionally uttering their guttural croaks.

Since ancient times raven has been known as the keeper of magic. Listen carefully to his voice. He brings guidance from a higher place. In the past, humans observed and listened to signs from animals precisely because of this capacity to give us the wisdom we need to find our way in life. Pay special attention to raven, who has a strong connection to higher powers and primordial forces. As a messenger between worlds, raven has the function of the shaman, who will journey to the spirit realm and bring back information to help restore balance on earth. If you observe raven, you will notice that he is very communicative. As he flies overhead, he seems to be commenting on what he sees. Raven is a highly intelligent bird and a master of language.

Once ravens have found a mate, the two remain close companions for life, and they can live for 50 years. They are private birds, roosting in pairs rather than in big flocks. This adds to the mystery surrounding them.

Raven's deep black coloring absorbs the light of the sun, and he likes to soar high. In the Viking tradition, Odin had two ravens, thought and memory, who flew over the land by day and returned to him at night to report what they had seen. Legends from the southwest coast of Canada say that raven was cunning enough to bring back the sun when it was stolen from the world by a chief who wanted it for himself.

Along with his restorative role in the universe, raven can take on the part of trickster, who creates problems for Earth's inhabitants. This double role may seem a paradox, but on the level of soul and spirit, the rational thinking and logic of our minds are not enough to understand the purpose and mystery of human existence. Humans harbor both destructive and beneficial forces. We need the trickster in order to be tested and challenged. We learn and grow through these tests and difficulties, and they are all part of the divine plan in which raven plays an important part.

Owl

* INTUITION * WISDOM * HUNTER

EARLY IN THE MORNING I walked down to the lake for a swim, out in the Finnish wilderness. I was guiding a group of English people on a kayaking trip, and we had camped for the night on an island covered with birches and pines.

As I stood by the edge of the water, enjoying the stillness, I heard a branch break behind me. I turned, expecting to see an animal between the trees, and to my surprise I discovered an eagle owl staring from its perch. Its large yellow eyes pierced me deeply with a presence that remains strong to this day.

The owl is a creature of night. Her flight feathers are covered with a velvet-like edging, enabling her to fly soundlessly. She is fully in the present, and like weasel, she will see what is hidden to others, however well it may be concealed. Some native people call her "eyes of the night." Her extraordinary hearing and vision register everything around her. Owl's voice travels far, telling of the mysteries of dreaming and the feminine. Owl medicine can be used to invoke these qualities. She signifies introspection, and having looked deeply into the dark and witnessed its secrets, she is a keeper of wisdom. Owl can see in all directions, her

neck allowing her to swivel her head 180 degrees both ways. Owl medicine allows us to use all four directions, and call upon the combined power of mind, body, spirit, and emotions. Usually people become strong in one of these areas, perhaps two. It is a high art to master all four. This is part of owl's wisdom. If owl's presence frightens you, go into the dark and find out its secrets. Take hold of your power and learn the wisdom of owl.

Big owls are sometimes called Wind Tigers. They are the stalkers of the sky, traveling in silence and striking their prey with flawless precision. The signs of their kills are scattered over the forest in the form of regurgitated pellets, returning the bones, hair, and feathers of their prey to the earth.

Owl has the courage to face threat without retreat. Whereas hawks, falcons, and eagles usually leave before you get a chance to approach them, owl waits to see if you will discover she is there, and if you do, she will face you, letting you know you have intruded onto her territory. One night as I was guarding a vision quest, my back against a beech trunk, two owls landed in the tree opposite me. They gave me a territorial glare. Then one of them flew at my face and

changed direction just before striking me, its feathers brushing the top of my head. Next it hit a dry branch that fell down and whacked me on the head. I got the point.

The next day I devised a ceremony of peace-making for the owls, and they let me be after that. But we still heard their hooting, carrying the wisdom of the night.

HAWK

✳ MESSENGER ✳ PRESENCE ✳ PRECISION

WHEN DESCRIBING HAWKS, I include American hawks and the English buzzard, which is very similar to the American redtailed hawk.

Having stalked quite a few animals, I always thought it would be amazing to have the chance to stalk a hawk, but never thought it would happen. Then what seemed like the perfect opportunity presented itself one windy summer's day. The hawk was sitting still, resting on a branch of a beech tree that was overlooking a lake. I approached from behind him, placing my feet silently and slowly on the ground. In spite of my efforts, the hawk suddenly swivelled its head and gave me one fierce look before taking off and gliding on the wind.

Hawk is always alert. Nothing escapes his sharp eyes. He teaches us to pay attention to what goes on around us. Concentrating on the present moment is to expand our awareness, and this opens the door to experiencing life more fully. We are born to live this reality, not to float. Call on hawk if you need to deepen your understanding of this.

Hawk is a hunter and a warrior. He soars high and can see everything below him. When he finds his prey, he strikes with precision and power. But although this skill is innate, hawk needs to hone it through practice. The young hawk misses his prey many times before he eventually begins to master the art of hunting. Hawk says: practice and you will be able to hunt down and strike what you really want in life.

Hawk's scream pierces the air and makes us look up, reminding us that we too can let our spirit fly, and we can achieve our full potential. Hawk brings us this message from the ancient ones, the great teachers who have guided humans through the ages.

CRANE

ATHIN MIST ROSE from the surface of the lake in the early morning as I was kayaking high up in the far north of Scandinavia. From the shore close by sounded the trumpeting song of the cranes. I could just about discern the outlines of their tall, grayish bodies as they merged with the mist. Later that morning, a group of five cranes flew right overhead.

The supernatural song proclaims good news, since crane keeps the wisdom of the divine. Standing on one leg, crane is always in balance, and she can keep this position for a very long time as she meditates, motionless, looking into the distance.

Crane has an ethereal presence. Her long legs and neck lift her whole body up toward the heavens, and the ease with which she can lift herself off the ground in spite of her large frame gives the impression that she is not restricted by gravity.

During the mating season, male and female crane perform a beautiful and intricate courtship dance. Crane teaches us to celebrate life and love, and to live life to the full. Cranes are known for their patience, and they are masters of living with grace. Ultimately, if we can live with grace we can also die with grace.

Cranes live in tundra and wetlands where they feed on toads and other creatures that are toxic to many mammals and birds. Most cranes have a red spot on the top of their heads, and legend has it that this is where all the toxins they have eaten are stored. Thus crane teaches us that we can transmute toxicity into beauty. Thoughts and emotions that often poison the hearts and minds of humans can be transformed and, in so doing, connect us to the divine.

OSPREY

A CLEARING BETWEEN two birch trees allowed me a view of the lake. It was noon, and the second day of my vision quest in Lapland. Everything around me was quiet.

There was a sudden rapid blur and a thump, as a fish fell from the sky and landed 3 ft—about a meter or so—in front of me within the small defined circle of my chosen spot. Astounded, I looked up, and caught a glimpse of an osprey flying off. His talons had pierced the fish lying in front of me. A vision quest is supposed to be undertaken in a state of fasting, so instead of cooking it I placed the fish on my altar and meditated on the meaning of that unexpected event.

Osprey are large hawks living primarily on fish. From high in the air, their sharp eyes detect movement under the water. Waiting for the right moment, osprey dives earthward like a lance and strikes with precision. Lifting himself up, surfacing from the water, he holds the fish secure with two talons in front and two behind, enabled by a reversible toe he has at the front of each talon. He flies off to the nest, where the female incubates her eggs in breeding season.

Osprey teaches us to see what is under the surface and to go deeper when we look for the things that can give us nourishment. Fish represent knowledge, wisdom, and spirit, so osprey urges us to leave behind the comfort of our familiar element and take the risk of diving into the water of knowledge. Here in the depth of the subconscious waits that which can feed our spirit. Osprey also tells us to pursue the things we want, and to strike with power when the time is right. Timing is everything for the hunter.

Osprey's reversible toes create a circular arrangement of his talons when seizing a fish, where the tips point to the four directions, forming the circle of life, or the medicine wheel. Osprey shows us that we need the power of all four directions representing body, mind, spirit, and emotions, in order to find our center. If we stay in one realm because we are comfortable there, perhaps avoiding other realms, we will be out of balance. We must seek those aspects of ourselves that need strengthening.

Osprey always points the head of the fish he has caught in the direction he is flying. In the process of turning the fish to be head first while on the wing, on rare occasions he drops it.

Like osprey, you can give your knowledge purpose and direction. Point it toward your goals and use it to reach your dreams, and your flight will become more streamlined, wasting less time and energy. If you lose what you thought you had achieved, call on osprey to inspire your sense of purpose to dive back into the water and seize another opportunity, just as he returns to catch another fish if the first eludes his grip.

EAGLE

ONE HOT AFTERNOON I was driving through the Nevada desert, down highway 50, which is reputed to be the loneliest highway in the USA. I hadn't seen another car for over an hour when I caught sight of something blocking the road ahead of me and began to brake. As the car slowed, I saw it was an eagle, standing in the middle of the road. I came to a halt 10 feet from it. The eagle's outstretched wings covered most of both lanes and in his talons was a rabbit. That eagle gave me the fiercest look I have ever seen.

Eagle's sharp eyes see over seven times more acutely than the human eye. His heart is strong. Golden eagles are known to have taken grown wolves. When hunting, eagle flies low and like an arrow, striking his prey with long talons. Like falcon, he shows us how to succeed through complete focus on the task. Our heart must be in our actions. He is the warrior of the sky, defying gravity as he soars higher than any other bird, up into a vast space that opens onto the universe, that mysterious realm, which we strive to access.

Everything about eagle is light. His neck is the color of gold. When he circles higher and higher, he and the sun seem as one; he rises into the world of spirit.

Eagle is the sunbird, the messenger between creator and creation. If he appears to us, we must listen, because he brings a message from the highest place. Traditionally his feathers were earned through courage and selflessness, and it is an honor to own one. Shamans use them for healing.

One of eagle's medicines is perspective. He sees both sides of the mountain and knows both sides to a story. If you are caught in a limited way of seeing things, call on eagle to broaden your horizon.

There is a downside to eagle medicine: if you stay up high, you can become aloof and separate from life. Eagle is not so sure-footed on the earth, but he must always come down from his airy realm, to sit on cliffs or in the branches of trees.

HERON

GLIDING TOWARD THE MOUTH of an estuary in my kayak, I noticed a heron standing by the shore among some birch saplings. He blended in perfectly. Standing on one leg, he was completely motionless, his long, pointed beak dipped just below the water's surface. I kept watching as I let the current carry me downstream. Suddenly, the heron came alive in an explosion of movement, his beak spearing through the water into his prey.

Heron is very quick when he strikes, but most of the time he moves with deliberate slowness, and he is not rushed. This is reflected in his leisurely wing beats, and the slow movement of his legs. He stands in the water, but with his long neck, his head is high in the air. He strikes a balance between feeling and mind. His small eyes see with clarity, which is a powerful mental state.

Heron has the patience and self-control to remain still for a very long time. He has the quietness of mind to be utterly focused. These are the gifts of a guardian, who allows nothing to pass unnoticed. Native people would train themselves in this manner. The mind of the human wants to wander and drift in multiple directions with the current of random thoughts. The mind is an amazing faculty and a useful servant, but if we let it be our master, it can become a tyrant. Heron has a different message: take charge of your thoughts and direct them. Learn how to choose them rather than following them blindly.

When heron stands still at the edge of the water, he sees his own reflection and he knows who he is. When we know ourselves, we can begin to accept ourselves; when we accept ourselves, it is easier to appreciate ourselves. When we appreciate ourselves, we respect ourselves. Self-acceptance is mirrored in the dignity with which heron stands between the water and the earth, between the realms of emotion and the physical.

Being yourself is an act of power. We can often spend a long time trying to be something or someone we are not. That is a difficult path to walk. Being yourself is much more fulfilling.

Perhaps you have been following a path that is not your own but that of someone who wields influence over you, or someone you admire. It is time to stop. Be still, like heron, look into the clear water of your deep self. See who you really are and where you need to go.

Although it is vital to look within, this is just the beginning of a process. We don't discover ourselves simply through sitting still and thinking. Neither does heron stand still continually. We also need to go out into the world and try different experiences.

Heron often spends a large part of the day by himself, and then returns to the colony, his community, at night. If heron has come to you, perhaps you need both reflective solitude and action within your wider community.

GOOSE

✳ SOUL ✳ LEADERSHIP ✳ GUARDIAN

SITTING BY A LAKE SHORE in Denmark as it grew dark one evening in fall, I heard the sound of geese behind me in the distance. Their honking grew louder and louder as they approached, and the thickening beat of their heavy wings, whipping the air, engulfed me. I sat perfectly still as they flew low over my head, and landed with noisy splashes on the water.

Geese can fly through air, swim in water, and walk on land. When they migrate, they fly at night. They are like our souls, which can leave the body during the night to travel in all elements and visit faraway places. The honking of geese is a call to us to remember who we are, to find our true selves, something we can only understand at soul level.

Migrating geese fly in a V-formation, taking turns to lead the flock at the point of the V. Goose teaches balanced leadership: one person, in charge of a task in which he or she has some expertise, does not lead permanently, but steps back and lets another take over. Many native tribes used the same system of leadership, which helps to create a circle of equality and makes the abuse of power less likely.

When wild geese land to graze, some birds stand guard. With their heads held high, they watch for any danger, ready to alert the rest of the flock if necessary. Domestic geese are also known to guard people and property. If intruders, human or animal, enter a garden or farmyard, geese will sound the alarm. They are considered to be at least as good guardians as dogs.

Another trait that distinguishes geese is the close bond that they build with each other. When they mate, they choose a partner for life.

WATER
ANIMALS

Water is feminine in its nature, present in both men and women. It is life-giving, fertile, nurturing, healing, and cleansing. People still seek holy springs in order to drink the healing waters, follow a pilgrimage to sacred rivers so that illness may be swept from them in the flow of life-blood, and pray for purification in the steam of sweat lodges. Life came out of the waters in the beginning of time and life grows in the water of the womb before emerging into the world.

Water holds the powers of trust and provision. It is connected to emotions and the strengths and dangers that come with them. In its essence, water is flexible, fluid, changing, moving, and absorbing. When encountering obstacles, the water of a river uses its flexibility to move around them; but eventually water will overcome just about anything. When you look at canyons that have been created by rivers cutting through solid rock over long periods of time, you begin to understand the power of water.

The changing quality of water is displayed in its ability to transform itself from liquid to frozen, from solid matter to steam that drifts on the wind. However, water will always be water, just like emotions. This is good to keep in mind: emotions cannot be changed into, for instance, thoughts. They must be accepted and dealt with.

SALMON

✳ REBIRTH ✳ PLENTY ✳ WISDOM

WHILE RIVER-RAFTING IN northern California, we descended a waterfall and afterward I went and sat on the riverbank to look at the water cascading down from the cliffs above. That's when I became aware of a huge salmon surging upward from the bottom of the fall, sailing through the air and up the wall of water. Its heavy body was close to three feet long, but it flew through the air, disobeying gravity. Then many others followed.

Each year salmon travels up the river against the current, journeying to her birthplace to lay her eggs. In North America

she dies after having spawned. This journey against the flow, the river of life, represents the soul of the dead, returning and bringing back life. When the eggs hatch, the young salmon swim back out to sea with the river's drift, and one day they too return. Salmon shows us that life on earth is a cycle of birth, death, and rebirth. We return until we have learned what we need to learn on the river of life. Each one of us must find our path and keep going until we reach our final destination.

Salmon teaches that even if there are difficulties, waterfalls along the route, you should never give up but keep taking leaps of which you might not have thought yourself capable.

The huge number of salmon traveling upriver each year provides food for bears, eagles, foxes, and humans. Salmon's gift represents the abundance and plenty of Mother Earth. In Finland, I was told that woodsmen used to request a guarantee in their contracts that they would not be served salmon every day, but for four days of the week only!

In Celtic lore, salmon lived in a spring by an oak tree. They ate the acorns that fell into the water, absorbing the oak's wisdom.

DUCK

✱ ABUNDANCE ✱ PLAY ✱ FEELINGS

I USED TO GO OUT to a pond in the wood near my home at dusk. I crouched by the trees and waited for the wild mallards and teal. I knew them by the pitch of the whistle their wings made as they flew in from the broad lake where they had spent the day. Teal were faster, their whistle more shrill. The wild ducks circled a few times over the pond, to make sure it was safe. Then they descended, landing with a hushed splash.

Duck has very strong connections with water, which gives life and sustains growth, so duck's medicine is abundance. If you have ever eaten a duck egg you will know how rich they are, and the same is true of the duck itself. A duck's body has a layer of thick fat under the skin.

Duck's close link to water is mirrored in her form. She can fly, but she doesn't soar like an eagle does. Eagle merges with the element of air while duck is denser and heavier, like water. Many ducks need to run along the water, paddling furiously, before they can take off from the surface tension and fly. Their heavy bodies take them down into the water, where they find food at the bottom of ponds, lakes, and rivers. Duck

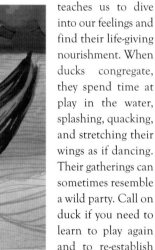

teaches us to dive into our feelings and find their life-giving nourishment. When ducks congregate, they spend time at play in the water, splashing, quacking, and stretching their wings as if dancing. Their gatherings can sometimes resemble a wild party. Call on duck if you need to learn to play again and to re-establish your ability to contact your true feelings.

Duck also knows the mysterious aspect of her element. She sometimes sits quietly between the reeds and listens to the song of the wind blowing though them, whispering the secrets of the water.

DOLPHIN

✳ JOY ✳ PROTECTION ✳ SEXUALITY

O N A WARM SUMMER'S DAY in Cornwall in southwest England, I was resting during my hike along the coastal path, lying flat on the grass and, from the clifftop, watching surfers in the waves of Sennen Cove below. A tall wave drew up, and a few surfers managed to catch it, starting their ride toward the shore. I suddenly noticed two dolphins arcing through the water, moving in closer and closer to the surfers. One of the dolphins, clearly visible in the light green of the wave's head, powered under a surfer's board and rode beneath him toward the shore.

During the next half an hour, the two dolphins swam slowly in and out among the surfers, sometimes coming very close to the boards, raising their heads to the water's surface, as if making direct contact with the people. When a good wave hit, the dolphins rallied. They sped through the water alongside the surfers, sometimes perpendicular to a board, and sometimes parallel with it, obviously having great fun.

One of the things we can learn from dolphin is to have fun for its own sake. For many adults, life tends to become very serious, and the ability to play is lost. Generally, adults are inclined to experience life through the mind and the ego; a shaman would say that they become caught in a bad dream of life. Dolphin teaches us to break free and keep a sense of deep joy alive within us. With that joy comes youthfulness and vitality, no matter what your age. Joy is a strong healing medicine on all levels of our being.

Some years ago, one of my teachers, an elderly Native American, was invited on a summer sailing trip in the Mediterranean. He and his hosts would often swim from the boat while it was anchored in the calm, warm water. One afternoon my teacher swam alone. About 50 yards from the boat, he began to have a heart attack. Nobody on board noticed. That was when a dolphin arrived and kept him afloat until he managed to get the attention of the people on board. He was rescued by them, but the dolphin saved his life.

Dolphins aid and protect, not only their kin but humans, too. They are very powerful hunters and warriors, and will fight and sometimes kill large sharks. They are also said to assist the souls of the dead in the crossing to the otherworld.

When dolphins surface, you will see that a spray of water spouts from the top of

their heads. They are mammals and have no gills, so they have to hold their breath when underwater. This spray is their exhalation, visible to the eye, reminding us that the breath of life is what keeps our spirit inside our body.

Like humans, and unlike most other animals, dolphins mate throughout the year. Highly sexual creatures, they remind us that life is created through union. If you choose, that union can be a way to raise your consciousness, ascending through love.

SWAN

* FLOW * GRACE * SPIRITUALITY

WALKING IN SUMMER through the woods in Norway, I became aware of a rhythmical whistling behind me. I turned and saw two swans flying low in my direction, the beat of their heavy wings causing that mystifying high-pitched sound. They landed in a pond up ahead, and I watched them from a distance, noticing how they transformed the landscape, making it easier for me to experience it deeply.

A swan on the water signifies the essence of effortlessness, command, and grace. Her long body appears to move unbidden, while she holds her neck and head with the utmost dignity. Swan teaches us to go with the flow of the river of life with as little resistance as possible. This way, when we allow ourselves to accept life as it is, we can permit events to unfold the way they are. By not resisting or judging what life brings us in the form of challenges, but rather seeing them as opportunities to learn and grow, we can align ourselves and be in harmony with reality as it presents itself. These are lessons carried in the feminine qualities of swan, in her grace and dignity.

Swan glides in pure white solemnity, and she can appear dreamy and otherworldly. These qualities, which she can also bestow on her surroundings, make her a keeper of the shamanic concept of dreaming. Swan flows in the Sacred Dream of Life. As a messenger from spirit realms, she is able to impart wisdom that can help us to awaken.

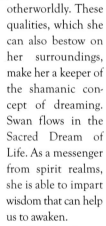

She is also a fierce and strong protector in defence of her boundaries, and those of her young, and her wings have been known to break human limbs. I have seen a swan fly along a river and attempt to board a small white motor boat in an effort to expel it from her territory.

WHALE

✴ HISTORY ✴ COMMUNICATION ✴ ANCIENT KNOWLEDGE

DRIVING UP HIGHWAY 101 in California, I came to a hilltop from where I had a clear view over the Pacific coast. I pulled over and got out of my truck. As I stood scanning the ocean, I saw a fountain of water burst from the sea, followed by the massive gray body of a humpback whale. Even when she dived under the surface, her dark body stood out against the blue water. It was like watching something from the beginning of time.

Life on Earth began in the oceans. Whale is ancient, and knows the history of planet Earth and its journey of evolution. Over time, she has adapted to live on land, then returned to the water. Whale travels thousands of miles in the great oceans and reaches depths inaccessible to humans. She sees previous worlds, whole continents, civilizations that have sunk in the water and disappeared from our memory. Thus whale brings insight into the instructions that were brought by the Great Teachers, who walked the Earth in times past.

Whales have individual songs, distinct from each other. The song of some whales can last for up to an hour, and then be repeated accurately. Whale can hear the song of her kin from a distance of a thousand miles. She knows the significance of sounds and words. Her primordial songs embrace the mysteries of creation. She teaches the secret power of language, and the importance of how you use words, because they create your reality.

Whale is a gentle mother, suckling her calves in the water and protecting them for several years. In many legends, whale swallows humans and then regurgitates them alive. Whale is truly like the Great Mother, holding all her children, traveling around the globe, and keeping her knowledge of the deep and of all time.

WATER/EARTH
ANIMALS

This group combines the movement and fluidity of water with the solidity of earth. The otter embodies these two powers; it moves with grace and speed in the water and is equally confident on the ground.

In the turtle we can see the solidity of the earth element in its protective shell, encasing its body almost entirely, yet turtle lives in the soft and yielding element of water.

Both water and earth are nurturing and life-giving, and if we contemplate them in more detail we see that earth mixed with water creates mud. Mud is a magical substance that provides the right condition for seeds to sprout and new life to emerge. For this to happen it also needs the air and the fiery sun. So life is really a dance of all four elements.

FROG

✳ SONG ✳ FERTILITY ✳ CLEANSING

HIGH UP IN the arid pine-covered mountains of Santa Cruz in California, the air was still warm late at night. I sat in the garden, listening to the rustling song of the corn plants in the soft breeze. Another sound gradually blended with them: the croaking of frogs from a little pond that a friend had constructed nearby a few years earlier. Their mesmerizing songs grew in strength and intensity, like a mysterious orchestra, and began to draw me into a very peaceful and altered state of awareness. The trees suddenly seemed enlarged, demanding my attention.

The deep resonance of frog's song carries us on spirit journeys, allowing us to enter other realities: she is a mediator between worlds. In some traditions, her song is perceived to summon water in the form of rain, which brings life and fertility when it hits the earth. Frog reflects this fertility in her abundance of eggs, which she lays in strings like fat raindrops. Frog's element is water. She teaches us to leap into the life-giving and purifying water that represents our emotions. Like water, emotions benefit us most when they are clean. Polluted with our own distortions, they can sometimes do harm. Frog's kinship with the cleansing quality of water means she is also associated with healing, and can be called on for this purpose. Her progress from egg to tadpole to frog represents the transformational journey we all go through as human beings in order to reach deeper understanding and develop as spirits born into substance. Sitting on a lily pad out in the middle of the pond, absorbing the sun's warmth, frog is chief of the water. She counsels us to trust, to take the leap, and to let the pure water cleanse us.

TURTLE

* PROTECTION * INTROSPECTION * STILLNESS

AT A UNIVERSITY CAMPUS in the Detroit area of Michigan, I stood by a pond and watched a turtle emerging from the water. She had just woken from winter hibernation, and moved incredibly slowly and dreamily as she swam over to a rock in the middle of the pond and climbed onto it. She positioned herself facing the sun and began to absorb its life-giving heat.

A turtle sitting thus, out in the water, is an image of North America. Many Native Americans refer to any land that resembles a turtle as Turtle Island. They say that Mother Earth is represented either by the back of turtle's shell, or by her flat stomach with her shell being the arc of the sky. Focusing on this symbolism, we can experience the Sacred Dream of Life.

Turtle's hard shell is a strong protection against enemies, and makes up for the fact that she is a very slow reptile who cannot outrun predators. When sleeping, her head is pulled completely inside her shell. Ask turtle for help if you need protection in order to feel safe in yourself.

Turtle rests within herself and does not have as much focus on the world around her as many other animals do. However, she has good eyesight and a keen sense of smell,

and is alert to what is happening around her at the same time as her awareness is predominantly turned inward. The fact that she carries her own shelter with her, as part of her body, emphasizes this introspective consciousness.

Call on turtle if you need to learn to bring your awareness back inside, rather than focusing all of it outside yourself. It is useful for us to do this in order to be truly centered. In western society, many people allow their awareness to be directed entirely outward, along the lines of what other people think, what television and radio broadcasting tell us. These things are part of our cultural communication and learning, but the continual direction of our focus outside ourselves does not always help us to see and act clearly. Turtle can guide you on how to bring your focus back to your core, and from this empowered position, turtle points out, you can become fully aware of what goes on around you, without losing your sense of self, trusting that you are protected.

The shell of turtle is like an aura, the energy shield universally perceived by shamans and spiritual teachers, which we always carry with us. Turtle teaches us to

build a strong aura through meditation and other spiritual practices.

Turtle shows us the wisdom of moving slowly, which we can do when we are centered, when the mind slows down to allow internal stillness. From there, we realize what is truly important in life, and we can begin to use discernment and choice in relation to what we want to do with our time.

PENGUIN

✳ RESPECT ✳ LOYALTY ✳ SUBCONSCIOUS

NEVER HAVING MET penguins in physical reality, I asked to see them in dreams, using one of the methods described earlier in this book. That same night I had an encounter with two little blue penguins. They were walking side by side and the way they moved in tandem spoke of strong bonds of trust and love between them. The sun was high in the sky, and their togetherness seemed to imbue the landscape around them with harmony.

Penguins return to the same location each year to breed. They show loyalty to the land of their ancestors, and they are also loyal in mating. Once they have found a partner, the couple stay together for life. Penguin as an animal spirit can assist you in integrating this quality of loyalty in your life.

Penguins live in extensive colonies, which sometimes number many thousands of birds. If you look at such an assembly, it seems amazingly well organized. In this, penguin teaches us to respect others. The main quality required for large numbers of individuals to function well together in a group is respect. For harmony and balance to be kept, and for conflicts between individuals to be dealt with quickly, properly, and effectively, respect needs to be an underlying principle.

The ocean is penguin's domain. Here she moves with grace and speed, hunting and finding her sustenance underwater. The ocean is a Great Mother who provides for her children, and is also the great subconscious to which we return every night in our dreams, feeding on the wisdom of the soul's deep water. Thus penguin is also a dream keeper. She knows how to leap effortlessly from dreams into waking life, just as she leaps from the waves onto the icy shore.

OTTER

✳ PLAY ✳ FEMININE ✳ GO WITH THE FLOW

I WAS WALKING alongside a stream in Cornwall, England, when I heard splashing coming from a point where the stream sloped steeply downhill, gathering momentum in little cascades as it wound through rocks. An otter was performing muscular leaps down the center of the stream, heading toward me. She bestowed a fearless, cursory glance in my direction as she bounded past me and continued her course downstream, her smooth body glinting with wetness.

Otter spends a lot of her time playing. She will slide down hills on her back in the snow only to run back up and have another go. Play and laughter are strong medicines, which sustain us when life is hard. Otter teaches her young to live their lives with an adventurous spirit, propelled by curiosity, daring to explore the world. Trust is a very important foundation for experiencing these qualities. It is the starting point from which everything else in us can blossom. When that otter bounded past me, she trusted that no harm would come to her. That is a great power to have. Otter can help inspire the feeling that you can handle what life throws at you and that other people are not a threat to be fought against, but equal companions with whom to share life.

Otter teaches us to flow with the current of life, to take it as it comes and deal with difficulties when they present themselves, rather than to live in a state of perpetual anxiety about them.

Otter balances two important realms of the feminine. As well as equanimity and grace, she can exhibit a striking fierceness. Otters will not attack but are known for their savage resistance to capture. She teaches that boldness is an integral part of feminine balance, that emotional flexibility is as much about the expression and use of inner fire as it is about the surrender of divisive rivalry. Otter's exuberant playfulness shows us that it is possible to embody these qualities and flow with trust in life.

BEAVER

* BUILDING * FAMILY * INDUSTRIOUSNESS

ONCE ON A WILDERNESS canoeing trip in southern Sweden, I paddled into a calm lake where the felled birch trees on the shore announced that I had entered the home territory of beavers. I paddled as silently as I could on the dark gray-blue water, hoping that I might catch a glimpse of one. After a few minutes I saw several beavers swimming up ahead of my canoe, their faces held above the water. They must have sensed my arrival: one of the beavers lifted her wide tail and slammed it down against the water's surface in a warning signal, and they all vanished immediately, not to return for some time.

Beavers create strong social structures. The family includes youngsters from the previous year, and they all live in dens constructed of trees and branches or in lodges below the water's surface, dug out from the bank. The entrances to these homes are under water. Beaver teaches the importance of family, relationship, and the strength of faithful union. Once beavers have found a partner and mated, they stay together for the rest of their lifetimes.

Beavers are skilled architects. Felling trees with their powerful incisors, they construct massive dams of the trunks and branches positioned across streams and rivers, all working together to create small lakes where the community can flourish. So beaver teaches that it's worth the effort to work industriously toward a goal you set for yourself, your family, or community.

Beavers are dedicated and very persistent, a lot like badgers. They will continue to work until the job is done. Beaver medicine brings the benefits of discipline in creative endeavor. Call on beaver to help you carry through your ideas with ingenuity and perseverance.

Beavers are slow on land, but once in water they are fast, elegant, and efficient. Their elemental home is traditionally the one most associated with emotions. Literally living under water for much of her time, beaver teaches the importance of being at home in your emotions. Emotions need to be acknowledged and given space. Like water, they can be nurturing, and if supported and contained, they can provide life-giving environments, like the lakes created by beaver's dams. Yet if the water upstream builds too strong a momentum and tears the dam apart, beaver simply starts again, not letting the past hold her back or sap her resolve.

SEAL

* SOUL * PROVISION * THRESHOLD

I WAS STANDING ON A Scottish seashore one summer's day, when I saw a seal raise its head above the water about ten feet away. The seal's big, dark eyes seemed to hold within them the very depth of the ocean. I was captivated. Those eloquent eyes seemed a metaphor for the human soul, which emerges occasionally from the depth of our psyche, showing itself for a brief moment, and then recedes again into the deep subconscious. Seal shows the way to reach our soul by diving into those depths, connecting with all that is hidden under the surface.

Seal's body is molded to life in the sea and appears to be a uniform mass without the clearly differentiated limbs that characterize land animals. To move and hunt in water with the utmost ease and mobility, it is as if seal has taken on the form of the sea itself, a vast expanse of highly flexible substance. The sea is the Great Mother who provides for her children, and seal in turn has provided for humans, such as the Inuit people, who live and eat in cold and hostile environments where it is hard to gather food. In this way, seal also becomes the Great Mother. Her rhythms are governed by the moon and tides. The milk with which she nurtures her young is extremely rich and high in fat content. It enables her children to develop a thick layer of fat, which they need to maintain their body heat in the freezing cold water.

Seal needs both land and water, and divides her time between the two. We too need time for worldly grounding, and time for the deep soul. Seal's medicine is that of "places between" where two different forces meet. Here we often find doorways, or thresholds, into the spirit world.

CHAPTER FIVE

ANIMAL SPIRITS AND YOUR LIFE'S PURPOSE

Along with being your protector, guide, teacher, friend, and companion, the power animal is closely linked to your purpose in life. Before many native traditions were destroyed by colonial invasions and religious interference, it was considered essential for every young man and woman to find their life purpose, assisted by their power animal.

When young people reached puberty, they began to seek dreams and visions that would clarify their direction in life. It was considered important that the fire within young people be channelled toward something useful, and this is still true today. The inner fire needs to be directed in positive and fulfilling ways. If young men, for example, cannot find a constructive direction for their fire they sometimes become destructive in the outer world.

Human beings need direction in their life to achieve a sense of fulfilment and so as not to become lost. Direction gives a sense of purpose, which awakens energy within us. If we have no genuine direction, dreams or visions for ourselves, we tend to feel low in energy, tire easily, and maybe even become depressed. If we have a sense of purpose, we get fired up and excited so that suddenly we have the energy to pursue what we want. You could say that purpose pulls us forward, giving us a sense of being alive. Children have dreams and visions and are full of vitality. However, adults who lose their direction tend to lose their vitality and sense of youthfulness, and therefore their enthusiasm.

INNER LIFE PURPOSE AND
WORLDLY LIFE PURPOSE

There are two categories of purpose in the life of a human being. The first is on an inner plane and involves learning certain soul qualities. If you look closely at your life you will discover that there is a theme running through it in terms of the lessons you receive. You may be here, for example, to learn about unconditional love, courage and moving through fear, generosity, trust, or compassion. Manifesting and integrating such qualities is our life purpose on the level of the soul. The second category is your worldly purpose: What are you supposed to manifest in the world in terms of profession and skills? This relates to your talents, your gifts, and how you bring them into the world. Ultimately the two life purposes are one. While this may not always be so in the life of a human being, it is more satisfying for us if it is.

Most people nowadays do not know the concept of a higher power having a purpose for them. Our sense of purpose is conflated with the achievement of certain goals we set ourselves. There is nothing inherently wrong with this. However, fulfilling your life purpose is not purely about becoming goal-oriented. When setting goals for yourself, keep in mind that your path should be your central focus. It is easy to become so focused on your set goals that your mind projects itself into the future, removing you from the here-and-now where life happens. Your immediate awareness and focus should be on each step you take on your path toward the destination. You are present and alive now, enjoying a path that will eventually take you home.

We can achieve goals incessantly but still be easily unsettled by events or by other people's behavior, and still feel unfulfilled on a soul level. Having goals brings us into the world but, without a strong foundation and balance of our inner energies, that exposure can leave us undermined. To dive into this work and make a commitment to it, I was taught to use ceremony.

FIRE CEREMONIES AND YOUR LIFE PURPOSE

Ceremonies allow us to transform and grow in ways that, if left to chance, might take a great deal more time and energy. In ceremonies you create sacred space by calling in supernatural help. In such an expanded space, doorways open and we achieve more than we thought possible. The timing needs to be right because ceremonies are to do with initiation, and we need to prepare ourselves first.

Of the many different types of ceremony I was taught, fire ceremonies are the ones most often used. My teacher said that fire was the first altar. Fire has long been the friend of humans, and it has an astonishing ability to transform. We can use fire ceremonies to transform qualities that are outdated and no longer serve us well, and we can use them to find our life purpose and begin to bring ourselves into alignment with it.

The fire ceremony below is useful for exactly this kind of work. As with all ceremonies, the power of your intention will affect how real the work becomes. The ceremony can be done at any time, but it is a good idea to work in alignment with the powers around you. For example, observe the phases of the moon, which traditionally people have worked with to let go of the old and call in the new. Sometimes people use the new moon to call in, and the full moon to let go of what is no longer needed. Sometimes the new moon is used for letting go. For me, the energy is always strongest at full moon, whether the purpose of a ceremony is to let go or to call in, so I would recommend doing the fire ceremony on a full moon.

Transformation through a fire ceremony

Find an appropriate location where you will not be disturbed. You might want to bring a friend with you who can act as a protector, to make sure you are not troubled by anyone. The ceremony could take place out in nature, but a garden is also fine. You will need to prepare the space by gathering wood, making a shallow fire pit, and finding stones to mark a ceremonial circle and the four directions within it. Build a small circle by placing a stone in

Opposite: A fire ceremony, when done at the right time, can help us to transform ourselves by letting go of the old, experiencing the emptiness that follows this letting go, and embracing the new.

each of the four directions: east, south, west, and north. Dig the fire pit in the center of your circle.

At the beginning of the ceremony, call on the seven directions and smudge your circle as described on page 40. Call on your power animal and ask for help. It can be useful to sing a song related to what you are doing. Light the fire from the east in a ceremonial way, then sit and gaze into it, letting it speak to you and guide you.

There are three parts to the ceremony: the first is to let go of the old, the second is to feel the emptiness once you have let go, and the third is to call in the new.

In the first part your intention may be to let go of any obstacle or block within yourself that holds you back from fully experiencing your life purpose. Begin by giving Grandfather Fire an offering of herbs, putting them on the flames, then telling him why you have come. Speak to

Having a Fire Ceremony

Intention:

✷ Letting go of what blocks you, and transforming it.

✷ Experiencing the emptiness.

✷ Awakening inner fire in relation to your life purpose.

You will need: Four stones, wood for a fire, a fire pit or the tools to make one, herbs for an offering and for smudging, an object for burning, and a piece of ribbon.

1 Prepare your circle and light the fire ceremonially in the east.

2 Call in the directional powers and your power animal. Ask the highest power for protection.

3 Give an offering to the fire, and speak to the fire about what you need. Then gaze into the flames, letting them speak to you.

4 Put into the fire the object representing your block.

5 Experience the emptiness of letting go of that block.

6 Gaze again into the flames while simultaneously traveling inward, awakening enthusiasm and true passion for qualities and talents aligned with your life purpose

7 Stand and claim your inner fire.

8 Tie a prayer ribbon onto a tree.

9 Give thanks and dissolve the circle.

Having had a real experience of the emptiness, move on to the final part of the ceremony. Now your intention is to awaken your inner fire, especially in relation to your life purpose.

Begin by gazing into Grandfather Fire, asking him to help you identify your deep enthusiasm, your disposition, and those qualities and talents that are in alignment with who you are. Ask the flames to help you call in and awaken the fire within yourself. You will need to quiet your mind, let go, and simply look into the fire, traveling inward to find your true passion. When you are done, stand up and claim your own fire.

him all about your life, who you are, and who you want to be, always letting your words come from the heart. Then ask Grandfather Fire to transform the block or obstacle within you. Put into the flames an object that represents what holds you back. As well as a symbolic object, it could be a piece of paper you have written on.

Now you must move on to the second part of the ceremony. This is when you will feel the emptiness that follows letting go. For this ceremony to succeed, you must truly experience the void at this point, even if it is only for a few minutes.

Step out of the circle and tie a ribbon or scrap of material to a tree. Let this be a physical prayer for the awakening of your deep enthusiasm and passion, and of the qualities and talents that allow you to carry out your life purpose in the world. The ribbon, now imbued with your prayer and intention, will whisper your request to the wind, and the wind will carry it in all directions so that the sacred powers will know.

THREE STEPS TO PERSONAL GROWTH

To me it is beyond any doubt that our ultimate life purpose is to become enlightened, but this task takes eons of time. Although the ultimate life purpose is the same for every one of us, each individual has his or her own purpose, too. According to the teachings I was given, this is because our past, and all that we bring with us on a karmic level, binds us. Each human has specific lessons he or she needs to learn based on past actions. If in the past we have judged other people who were not successful in the world, then maybe we need to experience ourselves what that is like, and in this way to learn compassion, too. Until we learn these lessons you could say that we are bound by our past. Those lessons will keep coming to us until we change. Our life purpose is very much about growth and, for growth to take place, we need to go through trials. Some of these can be severe and initially difficult to accept.

Opposite: Our individual life purpose is shaped by our past. Each one of us has lessons to learn, based on our past actions, and until we learn these lessons, it is difficult for us to move forward and to grow as people.

The following three tasks can help to clarify our life purpose, and are beneficial to our growth as individuals.

1: Overcoming obstacles and blocks

We need to identify and transform certain distorted qualities within ourselves that hold us back from fulfilling our purpose. Such qualities could, for instance, be selfishness, greed, envy, and certain kinds of fear. This work is an ongoing process, but it can be speeded up significantly through building a strong intention to change.

Discover what issues you need to overcome, then use them as stepping stones rather than habitually running up against them. Fear, for example, can be worked with, perhaps taking you on a journey of healing wounds from the past—a journey that, in itself, will take you closer to your life purpose. You may need help in this process, and that is part of the journey.

Begin to gather information about yourself. For this purpose it is helpful to seek a spirit animal that can help you hunt yourself, such as jaguar or panther. Without judging yourself, and with respect and compassion, objectively observe your own behavior and thought patterns, as well as your emotions and habits. How often do you spin off into emotional reactions? How often do you judge yourself? When do you judge others? When do you doubt yourself? By gathering this information, your mind is encouraged to develop along two lines. One part of you reacts as you normally would, and another observes and gathers knowledge about yourself from those reactions.

After practicing for a little while, you become capable of interrupting some of your emotional reactions and judgments because you have trained your awareness and made it stronger. Eventually you gain more and more understanding and control of negative reactions and thought patterns.

The ability to observe yourself with some objectivity is strengthened by your journey to find an appropriate spirit animal to help you, and by your trust that this spirit helper is the right one, because it has shown itself to you.

Carrying Out the Three Steps

1 Find the right spirit animal to help you hunt yourself. Then observe yourself compassionately over some time and identify what is blocking you. What are the obstacles keeping you from reaching your goals? Over time, do what is needed to overcome the obstacles, seeing them as stepping-stones. Seek help if you need it.

2 Using dreaming and the drum journey, begin a process of identifying, integrating, and finally transforming the hidden, distorted sides of the self.

3 With the help of dreaming, the drum journey, or fire ceremony, find a quality within yourself, related to your life purpose, which you are ready to work with. Use the shaman's energy cord method (page 48) to activate it.

Continue working to integrate this quality.

2: Integrating Distorted Energies

As human beings we all have certain images and beliefs about who we are that are not fully accurate because they exclude aspects of our character of which we are simply not aware. Our self-image might be that we are loving, kind, and caring, which is true most of the time, but then at other times we may act destructively. These are blind spots outside of our conscious awareness, which cause the same issues to confront us again and again.

With the dreaming exercises (pages 22–25) and the drum journey (page 29) we can begin a process of identifying these aspects of the self that are hidden in shadow. Bringing them up into the light, we can develop an awareness of them, accept, and transform them. This can be profound work for which you may need to seek guidance and assistance. It is a process of first observing, then interrupting, then directing the distorted energy toward useful tasks, and eventually making it an allied part of you.

Below: Dreaming exercises can allow us to identify the aspects of our characters that may be difficult to see by ourselves.

As with the work on obstacles and blocks, make identifications without blaming or judging yourself. View the process as a stepping-stone, rather than as any kind of obstruction.

3: Manifesting a specific quality or talent

Based on fire ceremonies, dreaming methods, and the drum journey, identify a quality or a talent within yourself that you are ready to integrate and bring fully into the world. You can use the method, The Shaman's Cord (pages 48–49) described in Chapter Three. Make this quality or talent the focus of your work and your intention, so that you gain a deep understanding of it and it becomes an integral part of who you are.

✦ Self-Responsibility ✦

All of the teachings outlined in this book point toward the strength and peace that come from knowing who you are and from being aligned with your purpose. Questions such as: "Who am I and what am I doing?" direct us back to the essence of what we are here for, and to clarity about what is really important.

This kind of self-knowledge should, according to the teachings, be accompanied by a prayerful attitude and a sense of humility like the one rabbit owns. True humility comes from knowing we are all drops in the ocean, and that we need support from the highest power in order to manifest our true purpose and to be fully ourselves in the world. This humility must be combined with a strong trust in our abilities, something that is learned in part from our power animal.

We can then walk in self-respect, remembering never to let go of this, no matter what life brings. Self-respect leads to self-authority and the certainty that you can make your own choices and do not need to give your power away to others. This can be followed by self-realization, a state of being genuinely yourself, bringing forward your gifts, and fulfilling your destiny. With that comes self-responsibility, meaning that you now are responsible for your own life and your own destiny. There is no expectation for other people to do the work for you or to take you where you need to be. You have your power animal, your gifts and strengths, and your direction and purpose. This awakens the remembrance of who you are. As you continue walking the path of self-respect and self-authority, animal spirits can show you the way.

Above: Dragonfly is keeper of potential, guiding you to fulfill your destiny.

✦ THE CIRCLE OF ALLIES ✦

We have seen in Chapter One how animals embody authenticity. Animal spirits are in harmony with nature and this extends to their way of being. They do not, for example, get angry without a reason. When we humans have an animal spirit by our side, it is easier to begin the process of overcoming the distorted sides of ourselves. Throughout, our animal spirits remind us of the qualities we are about to integrate in ourselves and manifest in the world. Each animal spirit has a different medicine, as described in the previous chapter, and it has limitations just as we do. Therefore it is very important to work with the right animal spirits for you. As human beings, we work on many different levels and in many directions at the same time, so we need to work with more than one animal spirit. As always, these animal spirits will choose us, rather than us choosing them. I was taught that there are usually four spirit helpers: The Circle of Allies.

Your power animal—your guardian spirit and a reflection of who you are—is one of the four. The three others will come to you as you seek them in dreams, drum journeys, and meditations. They have different medicines. One may be a good hunter, another may have the medicine of a strong family, the third may bring the quality of joy, and the fourth may bring focus and direction. Together, they will help you build strength in the different areas of your life. They can remain with you for a long time, sometimes even a lifetime. It might be that one of them leaves, in which case you would seek another to complete your circle again.

There is no rush to find all four animal spirits in your circle. In fact, it is generally a good idea to take your time, letting the search unfold in a natural, genuine way. This means the process can take a long time—it is often a good lesson

Above: The Circle of Allies is made up of four spirit helpers—one of which is your own power animal—and each one brings strength to the different areas of your life.

in patience and making sure that what you think is real. Remember that it is always your heart that knows what is real and what is not.

The sacred wheel

The Circle of Allies is so called because your four spirit animals take their places in the four cardinal points of the circle. As one animal after another finds you, you need to understand which direction it came from—east, south, west, or north. The best way is to let the spirit animal show you, but a basic understanding of the powers of the four directions is also helpful. These powers vary from culture to culture, and from tribe to tribe.

The ancestors from whom these teachings were passed down say that when you stand in a location that gives you a clear view in all directions, on top of a mountain or in a desert, you have a circle around you, and you are in the center of that circle. When you face the different directions you may sense that each one emanates, or evokes in you, a certain feeling or quality of energy. These energies define the powers of the four directions.

While there is no right or wrong way to work with the four directions, I recommend that you choose one system and stick to it, so as to not confuse yourself. Here is the model I work with:

Beginning in the east, move clockwise around the circle, with the sun. In the northern hemisphere, the power of the east is related to that of the rising sun. East is the place where light comes into the world. Here are the powers of vision and illumination. East is also the direction of the spirit. In the southern hemisphere, you can change the directions accordingly.

Moving clockwise around the wheel to the south, we find the place where the sun is highest in the sky, where warmth is greatest, and here we find the power of trust. This includes trust that you will be always be provided for, that whatever you may need is available. This power is connected to the emotions.

Moving to the west, we come to the direction where the sun sets. This direction pertains to darkness, without negative connotations. It means looking within. When you do so, you move inside your own body—the powers of the west involve introspection.

Now we move to the north, the source of cold wind. The cold wind brings clarity, wisdom, and strength—the powers of the north. It is also the place of the mind. This does not imply a purely mental faculty as it incorporates the ability to think with your heart.

When your animals take their places in this sacred wheel, they can begin to

Finding your Circle of Allies

1 Using dreaming, the drum journey, meditation, and prayer, begin seeking a circle of four animal spirit allies, including your power animal, which is your guardian spirit and a mirror of your personality. Take your time to find the Circle of Allies; it should be authentic.

2 Discover the position of your four animals in relation to the four cardinal directions.

3 Keep regular contact with the four animal spirits using the methods described in this book.

help you can contact throughout your life. If you need guidance for something that requires visionary qualities—your next step in life, a change of direction—then look to the east and ask that animal spirit for help. For a situation requiring deep trust and emotional adjustment, look to the south. If you are faced with challenges relating to your body, your grounding in life, or your inner knowledge, look to the west. For a challenge to your personal strength—for example, a choice that entails great courage, perhaps something you have avoided for most your life and are afraid of doing—seek help from the north.

The animal spirits at the four cardinal points guide you and create a strong foundation for you. The Circle of Allies does not exclude help for specific tasks from other animal spirits. Some may come to help you learn a certain lesson in life or to bring a message. A particular animal spirit might present itself to help you overcome a block or face something within yourself.

This is an introductory teaching about the Circle of Allies, and how to invite animal spirits to work with you and teach you their powers. The teachings can take you a long way on the journey of self-empowerment, raising consciousness, and awakening. Over time, the rest of the teachings may begin to emerge for you, too.

teach you more about their powers. Again, take time to let this unfold and remember that the process may not make sense from a logical perspective.

These directions and the four spirit animals become an invaluable source of

Index

abundance 71, 100, 129
adaptability 79
adaptation 81
aggression 78
air animals 59, 104-26
alertness 90
all-seeing 113
ancestors, in dreams 21
animal medicine 7-11
animal spirit helpers 43, 155-6, 157
animal spirits 18, 34, 58
animals 9-10, 17, 18
    authenticity of 32-3
ant 61
appreciation 82
architect 78
authenticity 32-3
awakening 103

badger 78
balance 85, 93
bat 111
bear 17, 43, 97
beauty 108
beaver 140
bee 104
behavior, of power animals 36
boar 83
boldness 68
bravery 83
breathing 40, 42
bridge, the 35
brotherhood 94
buffalo (bison) 100-1
building 140
butterfly 105

candles, for sacred fire 26, 28
cardinal points, four 26, 120, 156
cat 73
CD, shamanic drumming 26, 28, 29
centering 50

chakras 25
choice 9-10
Circle of Allies 155-7
clairvoyance 49
cleansing 135
clear mind, for dreaming 22-3
collective spirit 52
communication 133
community 61, 104
companionship 39
compassion 34
connection, feeling of 17-18
    with power animal 28, 29
cooperation 61
cord method 47, 48
Cosmos 26
council 112
courage 85
coyote 81
crane 119
creation 66
crow 112

dance 119
dancing, with power animal 28, 29
deer 90
depths, exploring 65
determination 100
dexterity 75
diet, and dream recall 23
dingo 79
distorted energies, integrating 153
dog 80
dolphin 130-1
dragonfly 106
dream induction 21-2, 24
    and intention 24-5
dream journal 22
dream recall 22-3
dream state, recognizing 51
dreaming 21-5, 64, 97, 111
    with power animals 40, 42
    and shape shifting 49, 50-1
drum journey 21, 26, 28, 29, 38

drumming 110
duck 129
duty 61

eagle 36, 123
earth animals 59, 60-102
elements, and animal spirits 58
elk 94
emotions 54-5, 63
energy 17
    integrating distorted 153
energy centers 47-8
energy conservation 89
equality 93
extra-sensory perception 18

falcon 113
family 77, 88, 140
feelings 129
feminine 139
fertility 83, 89, 135
fire ceremonies 146-9
flow 132, 139
focus 124
foresight 67
Four Daughters of Beauty 58
four directions 120, 156
fox 77
freedom 98
frog 135
frugality 93

gentleness 90
gifts, bringing 32
goddess 104
goose 126
grace 132
Grandfather Fire 148-9
Great Spirit 40
grounding 50
guardian 79, 80, 124, 126

hare 72
hawk 17, 32, 52, 118

Acknowledgments

It is an honor to be able to express my words in this book, one that I truly appreciate. On my trail through life I have met a lot of people, humans and others, to whom I am grateful. They are people who have had the courage to speak from the heart, listen from the heart, live from the heart, and they have all, in some ways, contributed to the book.

I am especially grateful to my teachers who shared their knowledge with generosity and sincerity; my students who have shown that they have a mind of their own; the animals who have always lifted my spirit and inspired me; the animal spirits for their friendship and ongoing help, loyalty, and integrity; Mother Earth for her unconditional love, my ancestors who are always there; and the Mystery for holding everything together. Finally, a special thank you to Zoë Bicât for all her help in shaping the text of this book.